a SAVOR THE SOUTH® *cookbook*

Bourbon

a SAVOR THE SOUTH® *cookbook*

Bourbon

KATHLEEN PURVIS

The University of North Carolina Press CHAPEL HILL

SAVOR THE SOUTH® is a registered trademark of the
University of North Carolina Press, Inc.
Designed by Kimberly Bryant and set in Miller and
Calluna Sans types by Rebecca Evans.

The paper in this book meets the guidelines for permanence and durability of
the Committee on Production Guidelines for Book Longevity of the Council on
Library Resources. The University of North Carolina Press has been a member
of the Green Press Initiative since 2003.

Library of Congress Cataloging-in-Publication Data
Purvis, Kathleen.
Bourbon / Kathleen Purvis.
pages cm.—(A savor the South cookbook)
Includes index.
ISBN 978-1-4696-1083-2 (cloth : alk. paper)
1. Cooking (Whiskey) I. Title.
TX726.P87 2013
641.2'52—dc23   2013008283

17 16 15 14 13   5 4 3 2 1

To my research assistant and always amusing husband, Wayne Hill, who makes sure I never have to rattle the ice in my glass too hard

Contents

a SAVOR THE SOUTH® *cookbook*

Bourbon

Introduction

THE LEGEND, LORE, AND

HISTORY OF BOURBON

elax. Sit back. Put your feet up if you like.

Now, pick up a glass—a stubby rocks glass, a rounded snifter, even a wine glass if that's all you've got. Pour in a splash of bourbon about as deep as the width of two fingers.

Take a gentle sip.

Taste that? It's wood and vanilla, smoke and caramel. Maybe even a hint, the slightest echo, of the sweet corn that started the journey leading to this brown liquid.

Add a drop or two of water, maybe a couple of cubes of ice. Notice how the bourbon opens up and tastes a little sweeter, how the flavors begin to fill your mouth.

Sip slowly, savor. And realize that what you're tasting is uniquely American and essentially southern. It's a creation that has splashed all over the map of America, but its origins are in the cornfields of Kentucky.

Bourbon has come into its own these days. Cult bourbons line liquor store shelves, and young chef/mixologists outdo themselves with ever-edgier bourbon concoctions. It's hard to believe there have been times when bourbon, America's greatest distilled creation, fell from favor.

In the 1920s, Prohibition burned through the South's great distilleries, emptying warehouses and putting hundreds of bourbon makers out of business. In 1919 alone, 52 Kentucky distilleries closed. Of 183 legal distilleries operating in that state at the beginning of Prohibition, fewer than half still existed to reopen after the repeal of the Volstead Act in 1933.

The whiskey world had a few decades to recover, and then came a second blow: the falling out of fashion of brown liquors like bourbon and Tennessee whiskey in the 1970s and 1980s. The vogue was to drink hipper alcohols, like vodkas with complicated names that no one could spell or pronounce and tequilas that came with bragging rights and mystique.

Bourbon? That was passé, something your dad or your granddad drank in a highball on a Saturday night.

Those days are certainly gone. In the 2010s, bourbon has made a triumphant return, a natural extension of the explosion of interest in locally grown foods and American craft creations. Roam the bar scenes in New York and L.A. today and you'll be hard-pressed to find a bartender who can't discuss classic bourbon cocktails that had almost disappeared—old-fashioneds and manhattans, juleps and sours. Chefs brag about their collections of rare bourbons that can run up to $60 for a single shot. Young hobbyists parse every detail of wheated bourbons versus rye.

With so many people enthused by bourbon, how did I get the job of capturing its story and its essence as an ingredient in the kitchen? I'm certainly a cocktail hobbyist myself, with an extensive collection of vintage books and bar gear on display in my home. I can weigh in with my own opinions on perfect manhattans and exactly how to muddle the mint in my personalized silver julep cup.

I think what really qualifies me, though, is perspective.

When I got interested in the art of cocktails, bourbon was not quite back in favor. As a newspaper copy editor in the early 1980s, I usually worked until late at night and would come home when there was nothing on TV but old movies. I drank in Myrna Loy and William Powell in *The Thin Man*, Katharine Hepburn and Cary Grant in *The Philadelphia Story*, and Marilyn Monroe leaning out of her train berth with a manhattan in hand in *Some Like It Hot*.

While watching these movies and their Prohibition-era drinking culture, I became captivated by the style and class of making a true cocktail. Putting together a cocktail was a craft, I realized, something that took time and effort to master. These weren't drinks you tossed back as fast as you could to catch a buzz before closing time. They were about enjoying liquor and life in a civilized way, by taking the time to sip and savor.

Before long, my husband and I had gotten our first silver-plated cocktail shaker—one of dozens that now grace our shelves—and we started digging into battered bar books pilfered from our fathers' collections.

While we certainly shook up plenty of martinis (gin, please) and daiquiris (never frozen), we tended to be drawn to bourbon drinks. Maybe that's because we're both southern—Georgia for me, North Florida for Wayne—and the drinks of our parents were highballs, whiskey sodas, and the lovely old-fashioned, with its festive cherry and orange slice.

Once we started to fill a liquor cabinet with a regular lineup of bottles, I also began to notice the classic southern dishes that had a taste of bourbon, from Christmas bourbon balls to the notorious Lane cake made famous in *To Kill a Mockingbird*.

In researching this book, I learned even more about cooking with bourbon—how to keep its flavor from being overwhelmed by other flavors or dissipating from heat, how to play to its strengths as a glaze or as a match for sweet and savory ingredients.

My husband and I went to Kentucky to see where bourbon started, and we went back through our collection of classic and historic cocktails to choose the ones we thought every bourbon fan—beginner or established aficionado—ought to try. We even came up with home-kitchen versions of a few of the edgier concoctions that today's mixologists are creating.

Along the way, we developed a new respect for that old brown liquor our dads knew. Bourbon isn't just something to drink. It's an artisan product that takes years to create. It's an American craft and a part of our history.

We should all raise a glass to that.

Born in Rock

As you cross the Tennessee border into Kentucky and head north on I-75, the rocks rise up around you. Sheer, solid walls of rock, so high beside the road that it feels like you're driving past fortresses, ridged with natural striations and stained in colors from gray and dun to steel and rust, even soft sage green.

Even after you pass through the mountains and into the rolling green hills of Kentucky's horse country, from Lexington to Frankfort and west toward Louisville, the rocks never disappear completely. Ridges push up through the grassy meadows and out from the shoulder of any road. As my husband mused on one drive: "This state wasn't built. It was carved."

If you're ever in Kentucky, take a good look at those rocks because they're a key component of the story of bourbon.

The rock is limestone, and a huge shelf of it, called the Cincinnati Arch by geologists, stretches for miles under this part of the world. Since it's porous, it provides natural filtration, creating pure water that's free of iron and sulphur. Without this water, early attempts to make bourbon would have ended up with a liquid that turned black and smelled nasty.

The limestone also contributes another benefit: As water trickles through the limestone, it picks up minerals, particularly calcium, that help yeast work better in fermentation. There's so much calcium in the water table that it even fortifies the grass eaten by horses, giving them stronger bones.

Apparently, there's a reason that bourbon and racehorses go together like bourbon and mint.

Bourbon: What It Is

What makes bourbon bourbon? It isn't place, exactly. While an estimated 95 percent of the world's bourbon is made in Kentucky, there's no rule that bourbon has to be made there.

Congress declared bourbon an American spirit in 1964. A substance can't be called bourbon unless it meets these rules:

1. It has to be made in America. You can make bourbon in Illinois or California or Virginia, and if it meets the other criteria for bourbon, it's bourbon. But if you make a corn-based, distilled, aged whiskey in Scotland or Japan, you can't sell it in America as bourbon.
2. It has to be made from corn, but you can combine the corn with other grains. All bourbon contains barley, which helps

the corn ferment, and either wheat or rye (we'll come back to the issue of rye). But the majority of the mix, at least 51 percent, has to be corn. For most bourbons, the percentage of corn actually is much higher, usually around 75 percent.

3. It has to be aged at least two years, although few bourbons are aged for such a short time. If it's labeled "straight" bourbon, it's aged less than four years and has to have the age on the label. Most bourbons are aged for at least four years, good ones are aged eight to ten years, and the really good stuff is aged more than ten years—and priced accordingly. The legendary Pappy Van Winkle line, made by Old Rip Van Winkle, includes a twenty-three-year-old bourbon that sells for more than $200 a bottle and resells for much more—if you can even find a bottle.

4. It has to be aged in new barrels made from American oak that are charred—lightly burned—on the inside. The long exposure to charred oak is what gives bourbon its characteristic color and complex flavor. It goes into the barrel as a clear liquid with a harsh, distinctive flavor. It comes out years later as a smooth-tasting brown liquor with hundreds of flavor notes, from vanilla to caramel to smoke and beyond.

5. It has to be distilled to no more than 160 proof, or 80 percent alcohol by volume; put into the barrel at no more than 125 proof, or 62.5 percent alcohol; and bottled at 80 proof or higher, or at least 40 percent alcohol.

You can't add any coloring or flavoring to bourbon. To correct the proof, you have to use only water or other bourbon. Besides "straight" bourbon, bottlers now also make single-barrel and small-batch bourbons, which usually come from a group of no more than twelve barrels.

So what's the deal with rye? If it's made in America and has "rye whiskey" on the label, it has to be made from at least 51 percent rye, along with corn and barley. Otherwise, it's made the same as bourbon, often in the same facility by the same distiller.

(Canadian rye doesn't have the same labeling standard and may not have been made from rye at all.)

Bourbons made with rye have a robust flavor with a spicy finish, while wheated bourbons tend to be sweeter. Some rye fans think it makes better cocktails than bourbon, although I think both have their place. It's worth tasting a rye manhattan and a bourbon manhattan side by side to see which one you like better.

One more thing: What happens to all those used bourbon barrels? They're handmade from carefully chosen American oak, and they don't come cheap. But by law, they can't be used again for another batch of bourbon. Instead, they're shipped all over the world to flavor other things—to Scotland for aging Scotch, to Ireland for aging Irish whiskey, to the Caribbean for rum. They even go to Louisiana for aging Tabasco, and some artisan food producers are using them to add flavor to things like beer and maple syrup.

From Still to Barrel

In our age of automation, it's inspiring to visit a bourbon distillery and see how much craft and nature are still involved in making this product. Bourbon truly is handmade, and no computer app can replicate it.

All bourbon starts with corn, barley, and rye or wheat. The corn is mostly grown in Kentucky, while the barley comes from Minnesota and the rye or wheat comes from Nebraska or other midwestern states.

The grains are delivered to the distillery and inspected to make sure they're free of mold and excessive debris from the fields. They're also checked for moisture—too much and the grains might germinate and spoil the mash. Farms that have contracts with distilleries are careful to deliver a good product, though: A distillery contract can be lucrative, guaranteeing a steady price for your crop for generations.

The Barton 1792 Distillery in Bardstown, Kentucky, makes 180,000 gallons of corn mash every week from mid-September through April, going through thirty acres of corn every twenty-four hours. If you were a farmer, wouldn't you want a slice of that business?

Every distillery handles its grains differently. Some combine different grains before they grind them; others grind and then mix them. They all have top-secret yeast strains, too. Different yeasts and different ratios of corn to barley can yield different flavors.

The basic steps in creating whiskey from corn have been around for centuries. First, you make a mash of corn, wet barley, yeast, and water. At many distilleries, such as Woodford Reserve, Maker's Mark, and Heaven Hill, the mash is still made in big cypress vats that look like backyard hot tubs full of corn mush.

The mash works quickly, converting the corn's starch into sugar so fast that the carbon dioxide it produces can drive oxygen from the air if you don't have good ventilation. When you look at the vats, they appear to be boiling, with big bubbles slowly rising and popping, like corn-colored La Brea Tar Pits. But if you stick a finger in the mash, it's surprisingly cool with just a hint of warmth. What looks like cooking is really fizzing, as the corn begins to ferment.

If you taste the mash right after it starts working, it's very sweet, like creamed corn. By the end, usually three days later, it has lost that sweetness and tastes like sour beer. At that point, it's called distiller's beer, among other names.

After the mash finishes working, it goes into one of two kinds of stills. There's the pot still, an ancient design that looks like a squatty acorn made of copper with a pipe coming out of the top. Woodford Reserve still uses three pot stills, made in Scotland.

Most distilleries, though, use the column still, also called a continuous still. A tower that rises five or six stories, the column still has a series of plates with holes inside. As the distiller's beer is heated, the steam of water vapor and alcohol rises. The plates catch the water, allowing the alcohol to continue rising to the top, where it is captured and cooled, emerging as distilled alcohol.

It helps to remember that stills don't create alcohol. They pull alcohol out of fermented mixtures and concentrate it by separating it from water—a.k.a. distilling. Understand that principle, and you can make alcohol in anything from a stack of tin cans to a copper pot in the woods.

But the alcohol you get is still pretty tough to drink. It's clear with an intense, almost oily flavor. In bourbon-making, it's called white dog, but you used to find it all over the South under other names, like white lightning or moonshine.

So there's one more step in the process: maturation or aging. How that's done is really what separates bourbon from every other kind of whiskey. The clear distilled alcohol goes into one of those charred oak barrels and is sealed with a wooden plug called a bung. The bung is usually made from poplar, the only wood besides oak that comes into contact with the whiskey. Poplar is softer than oak, so when it's time to open the barrel, a good whack with a mallet will make it pop out.

Then the barrels go into storage. But they aren't just stacked up any old place. The design and inner working of rickhouses—the warehouses that hold whiskey barrels—are as fascinating as the design of sailing ships. They even look a little like ships' holds on the inside.

Although rickhouses can be heated by steam, most of the climate control is provided by the weather and the design of the building itself. A typical rickhouse is five or six stories tall, with shuttered windows. The windows are opened and closed in a particular pattern to control moisture, sort of in the way that a ship's captain might regulate wind speed by raising and lowering sails.

One reason that an extensive tradition of making whiskey evolved in the South instead of in New England or the Midwest is the region's heat and humidity. Bourbon aging speeds up in the summer and slows down in the winter, allowing for the long, slow ripening in the barrels. At temperatures below 45 degrees, it goes dormant. Most distilleries only make new whiskey from September to April since excessive heat complicates cooling the tanks. Everything shuts down for the summer while the whiskey continues to age in the rickhouses as the barrels expand and contract, drawing whiskey in and out of the pores of the wood.

On the outside, rickhouses may be brick, wood, or even metal. They often have a distinctive black stain on the exterior of the lower floors. That's distiller's mold, which blackens everything from tree trunks to cars anywhere near a still. (It used to be one way federal agents located illegal moonshine stills.)

Once you go inside, though, all rickhouses look the same. They're cooler at the bottom, while at the top, temperatures can rise as high as 130 degrees. This creates different microclimates throughout each warehouse.

Inside, filling every floor, wood timber frames hold the big barrels. The barrels are rolled into place in precise patterns and are mapped to track the conditions in different parts of the rickhouse, so barrels can be chosen from different areas to make each batch.

With 52 gallons of new whiskey inside, the barrels start out at 550 pounds. They're so heavy that rickhouses have to be watched carefully for any signs of tilting. Look around and you'll always find a plumb bob hanging somewhere, checked regularly by the workers.

The other thing that's the same inside every rickhouse is the smell: a distinctive aroma of wood and whiskey that's called the angel's share. That's the smell of whiskey evaporating through the pores of the wooden barrels, and it really is heavenly. Because water molecules are smaller than alcohol molecules, what leaves the barrels is mostly water. That makes the alcohol left behind stronger and more intense in flavor, while exposure to the charred wood inside gives it color and more flavor.

After whiskey goes into a new barrel, it loses 10–12 percent of its volume in the first year as it soaks into the wood. After that, it loses a steady 3–4 percent a year to evaporation. For a whiskey aged four years, that means you lose roughly a quarter of the barrel. For a premium whiskey like Maker's Mark, 52 gallons go in and 35–42 gallons come out. Imagine a whiskey like the oldest Pappy Van Winkle: After twenty-three years, you get less than a quarter of what went in.

Oh, and did I mention the taxman's cut? As soon as a barrel goes into a rickhouse, it becomes a taxable asset. So the distillery pays a tax every year on whiskey that's disappearing into the air.

Do you still wonder why an eighteen-year-old bourbon costs so much?

How Did It Get Here?

So how did all these parts of bourbon manufacturing come together? Making alcohol has been around almost as long as humans have. We've always found ways to use yeast to turn various things into alcohol, for our nutrition and our pleasure.

Beer brewing is a fairly simple process. And if you take that beer and find a way to distill it, using heat and cold to separate alcohol and collect it, you can make something a lot stronger.

The knowledge of how to do that has been around a long time. *A Compleat Body of Distilling*, about the science of making what was originally called "usquebaugh," or whiskey, was published in London in 1731.

Before the American Revolution, making whiskey was already a regular plantation activity. George Washington made it and even sold it. Washington also may have encouraged the growth of whiskey-making as a business in Kentucky as an outcome of the Whiskey Rebellion.

Making corn whiskey was an established business in the 1790s, particularly in areas to the west and deep in the American wilderness where it was harder to get crops to market. Turning corn into whiskey was efficient and popular. In some areas where people had little access to cash, whiskey even functioned as currency.

By 1791, Washington, in search of revenue to pay off debts from the Revolutionary War, levied a tax on grain that had been made into whiskey. That tax hit people in rural areas particularly hard, causing unrest that came to a head in western Pennsylvania when troops were called in to enforce the collection of the tax.

It was an important test of the powers of the new federal government, involving the question of whether it could demand that a tax be paid and collected. Even though the government won, the whiskey tax continued to be unpopular throughout the southern states.

In Kentucky, though, the tax wasn't collected because local officials refused to do it and because farms there were so isolated. So some farmers had an incentive to move to Kentucky, where growing corn and turning it into whiskey continued without much restraint. It was particularly popular in Bourbon County, a remnant of what once had been a vast territory named for France's royal family that stretched from Virginia across the mountains.

Because corn has a shallow root system, it grows well in the hard, rocky soil around the southern mountains. It doesn't take much acreage to raise a good crop of corn.

And because you can do so much with it, you can build a whole world around a corn crop. Dry the kernels and they'll keep for months. Grind them and you'll get something like flour for making bread or a simple mush. Feed corn to your livestock and your children and they'll all grow big and healthy.

And if you grind it up and mix it with water and yeast . . . well, you get something you can drink that will make your hard days a little more bearable.

There's one problem with corn, though: It's heavy. A bushel of corn weighs fifty-six pounds, so a horse could only carry four to five bushels. But if you turned that corn into a liquid, it became much more portable. A flatboat or raft loaded with barrels could carry a lot of corn liquor.

If you were near a river, like the Ohio, you could steer that boat full of barrels to the Mississippi and down to New Orleans. It took months, but the price of corn whiskey in New Orleans made the trip worthwhile.

So a trade sprang up, with Kentucky whiskey shipped downriver in barrels stamped with their county of origin: Bourbon.

Wherever whiskey goes, exaggerated stories follow. So the next step in bourbon's evolution is less clear. According to legend, a minister named Elijah Craig is the father of bourbon, the man who discovered the secret of putting whiskey in charred barrels to give it color and flavor.

The favorite story is that Craig was a little tight with his money. So when there was a fire in his barn and some of his barrel staves got burned, he made them into barrels anyway, with the burned side turned inward so no one would know. (Maybe, maybe not.)

According to another story, Craig reused barrels, and he charred the insides to clear out any traces of the last batch. (Maybe, maybe not.) Or it could be that Craig was just an innovative guy. That's slightly more plausible—Craig was known for things like establishing Kentucky's first operation to make rope from hemp.

A more likely theory has nothing to do with Craig. European distillers already knew about aging liquor in wooden barrels, including charred barrels. So French customers in New Orleans might have planted the idea themselves by asking for whiskey that tasted more like cognac.

However it happened, people started to talk about that brown whiskey that came from the barrels stamped "Bourbon."

Cooking with Bourbon

Making cocktails with bourbon is easy. Cooking with it, beyond the basics of brushing a cake with bourbon or deglazing a pan, isn't that obvious.

While I was developing the recipes for this book, I called Sean Brock, the young Charleston chef known for food that embraces and reinterprets southern culinary history. Brock is also a known bourbon nut, one of those aficionados who has brought bourbon back to the forefront.

When I asked how he approaches cooking with bourbon, he declared that he doesn't. "When we cook with it, we don't apply heat to it," he said. "I'm such a bourbon fanatic, and I understand the work that goes into getting that flavor. Someone just spent ten to twelve years putting that flavor in it." Too much heat, he said, and you'll lose that distinctive flavor.

Instead, Brock looks for ways to use bourbon in food in its raw form. "Preservation and aging and time and patience—those are words that mean a lot to me."

Then he laughed: "I'm no help at all to you, am I?"

Actually, he did help me. He freed me up to accept something I already had discovered for myself: If you're going to use bourbon in food, you have to let the bourbon taste like bourbon.

Sure, there are some cooking uses of alcohol. I love to use bourbon to deglaze a pan or simmer into a smoky sauce with notes of caramel, vanilla, and orange. It plays beautifully with honey or Asian sauces, particularly hoisin and soy sauce. But if you really want to keep the character of bourbon, you usually have to work some raw bourbon into the dish.

To keep the bourbon from thinning out mixtures, I often cook things to be a little thicker or I include something—usually sugar or fat—to which the flavor can cling.

One cooking method I avoided, though, is flambéing. First, it takes away the bourbon's flavor. Rum and brandy make better-tasting fuels because of their residual sugar. Second, I find that many home cooks are nervous about deliberately setting something on fire in the kitchen. So I skipped that method here.

Because bourbon has so many flavor notes, though, you can take it in almost any direction. It has smokiness and earthiness, a peppery character, a natural sweetness, and a caramel, vanilla flavor. It loves oranges and apples, and it plays well with mushrooms and wild salmon. I discovered bourbon dishes with chicken, beef, and pork.

Which bourbon should you keep in the kitchen? Rather than get too obsessed with the flavor notes of wheated bourbons versus ryes, I like to cook with a standard bourbon that's reliable in flavor and reasonably priced. Why cook with something that costs $30 or $40 a bottle?

After a lot of experimenting and comparing, I decided that my kitchen bourbon of choice is Evan Williams Green Label. You can get a generous 750ml bottle for around $14, but it's well made and not harsh. Another I like in the same price range is Very Old Barton's. If you end up trapped in the kitchen and have to drink your bourbon to survive, either one of those will be there for you.

Don't Keep It Bottled Up

Bourbon distilling is a big business, and the distilleries around Kentucky make a big business out of bringing in fans for tours. Most are historic properties that are well maintained and prettified, offering an efficient hour-long look at the business that always ends right on time with a tasting in the gift shop.

Our afternoon at Buffalo Trace in Frankfort, owned by the Sazerac company of New Orleans, was a little different. We signed up for a behind-the-scenes tour, and we ended up in the hands of a bourbon expert named Freddie Johnson.

Johnson is the third generation of an African American family that has worked for many years at the sprawling facility on the Kentucky River, which became Buffalo Trace when the Sazerac company bought it in 1992. When his grandfather and father worked there, it was still the George T. Stagg Distillery, a name that dates to the 1870s. But distilling at that location has gone on much longer, at least back to 1773.

During Prohibition, Stagg was one of the few distilleries in the country that was allowed to continue making whiskey for medicinal or culinary purposes. The rickhouses still have bars on the windows and double locks on the doors. During Prohibition, a federal agent kept one key and the distillery owner kept the other, so they always had to go in together.

Today, Sazerac makes thirteen bourbons at Buffalo Trace, including Blanton's, Eagle Rare, and its own Buffalo Trace line, as well as aging Old Rip Van Winkle's Pappy Van Winkle. (Sazerac also owns Barton 1792 in Bardstown, where it makes six more bourbons and bottles a number of other liquors and cocktail mixes.)

With brick buildings, steam pipes, and tracks to move barrels all over the grounds, Buffalo Trace looks like a factory from an old Warner Brothers movie, right down to having a big water tower with an American bison painted on it. If you want to find someone who seriously loves every bit of the minutia of bourbon-making, you need to spend a few hours with Freddie Johnson.

As a boy, he played in the rickhouses and ran all over the property. Today, he knows every inch of the place, and he's fond of spouting enigmatic lines like "An oak tree is to bourbon what a grapevine is to wine," and "Corn is to bourbon what corn syrup is to pecan pie."

When we explained our book project, he spent more than three hours hauling us all over the plant in a golf cart, from the assembly line where workers were carefully hand-labeling bottles of Blanton's to the rickhouses, which he claims are haunted.

We watched "the barrel dance," in which aged barrels are rolled down a sloping track into the building, where they're emptied into screened sluices. Since the barrels have lost so much whiskey, their contents slosh as they roll down the track, causing them to wiggle from side to side, so workers run beside them to keep them on track, as if chasing fat wooden pigs into pens.

Retired workers like Johnson's father passed on labor-saving tricks used at distilleries years ago. For instance, we watched two workers unload a truck of empty barrels. Instead of lifting each barrel off the back of the truck and carrying it to a storehouse, they placed an old truck tire on the ground behind the truck. Then one man stood on the truck and dropped each barrel down onto the tire while a second man stood beside the tire. When the barrel hit the tire and bounced up, he batted it, sending it flying toward the storage building. It was like watching a giant game of tiddly-winks, and from the grins on their faces, it was just as much fun.

Johnson took us up through the levels of the column still, letting us taste the mash in the vats and the white dog dripping into a decorative copper and glass box at the top called the tailbox, where the master distiller checks samples. At the very top, we climbed out onto an iron platform to admire the spectacular view.

Johnson took us into one outbuilding where several barrels are on display with the ends replaced with glass so you can see how the whiskey has disappeared from the barrels.

Because of the time bourbon takes to age, Johnson said, a bourbon maker might only make three great barrels in a lifetime, getting to taste the result twenty years later.

"If time was not a factor in our lives, this is what we could enjoy every day," his father used to tell him.

One of his father's proudest moments was the day they filled the millionth barrel with whiskey and rolled it into a rickhouse.

Johnson moved away from Frankfort after he grew up, but a few years ago, when his father and brother both had cancer, he returned and got a job leading tours and tasting seminars at Buffalo Trace. When his father was nearing the end of his life, Johnson decided to track down a bottle from that millionth barrel. He took it to his father and brother so they all could drink a toast together.

After pouring a drink for each of them, Johnson started to recork the bottle. It was so old, so precious.

His father stopped him. "A bottle is meant to be drunk," he said. So Johnson put down the cork and they sat for three hours, sipping and relaxing together. It was the only time Johnson ever had to put his father to bed. But it was worth it, he said, to experience bourbon the way it is meant to be experienced.

"Don't rush it," he said. "It's so concentrated with flavors, more than 300 of them. Give them time to warm and break down. Talk and let it breathe."

After all that work to get bourbon in a bottle, don't just keep it there.

Open it, drink it, mix with it, cook with it.

It was made to be enjoyed.

Bourbon Cocktails and Other Imbibe-ables

There are probably hundreds of drinks that include bourbon. But the classics became classic for a reason—they're the ones that are so perfect, we keep going back to them. This chapter features the ones that I think any bourbon fan should know, including the "holy three"—the old-fashioned, the manhattan, and the mint julep. There are newcomers worth embracing, too. I've come up with home versions of new specialties, such as Bacon Bourbon and Smoked Bourbon. Maybe someday they'll be classics, too.

Smoked Bourbon

I knew bourbon had caught the attention of a new generation of mixologists the first time I had a smoked mint julep at a restaurant. But since restaurants have access to special equipment like gun-style smokers, I thought this would stay out of reach of home bartenders until I discovered how simple it is to smoke bourbon on a charcoal grill. The trick: Keep the fire low to reduce evaporation, and put the bourbon in a wide pan to expose more of it to the smoke.

MAKES ABOUT 3 CUPS

About 2 cups hickory chips
6 cups bourbon, divided
1 cup water
About 2 quarts charcoal, or about 30 briquettes

Place the hickory chips in a bowl and cover with 1 cup bourbon and the water. Set aside for at least 30 minutes. Pour the remaining 5 cups bourbon into a wide, flat pan, such as a 13 × 9-inch baking pan.

Set up the grill for indirect heat, with a rack on one side and an area for hot coals on the other. If you can, open the top and bottom grill vents on the side with the area for coals.

Ignite the charcoal. I prefer using a charcoal chimney instead of lighter fluid. To reduce evaporation, you don't want a large fire, so use only enough charcoal to fill the chimney about half full. When the coals are completely covered with white ash, spread them in the grill to create a low fire.

Place the pan of bourbon on the rack opposite the coals. Add a handful of soaked hickory chips to the coals and cover the grill. Smoke for about 1 hour, adding more hickory chips every 15 minutes.

Remove the pan of bourbon and cool completely, then pour into a jar or bottle with a tight lid.

USES ❋ To make a smoked mint julep, simply follow the Classic Mint Julep recipe (page 25) using Smoked Bourbon. Or use half Smoked Bourbon and half Bacon Bourbon (page 20) for a truly sublime Bloody Mary.

Bacon Bourbon

Making a bacon-infused bourbon is simple if you know about an old method of flavoring alcohol called fat-washing. Fat carries flavor, as anyone who has tried to reduce fat in their cooking has noticed. If you transfer a flavoring to fat and then put it in contact with alcohol for a little while, you can make a flavored alcohol.

MAKES 2 CUPS

5–6 slices thick-cut bacon

2 cups bourbon

Place the bacon in a preheated heavy skillet over medium heat. Cook slowly to render the fat, reducing the heat if necessary to keep from burning the bacon or the fat. You should have about ¼ cup bacon fat. (If not, cook more bacon.) Set the bacon aside for another use.

Place the bourbon and bacon fat in a jar with a tight lid. Let stand 18–24 hours, swirling the jar occasionally to bring the bourbon into contact with the fat.

Place the jar in the freezer for 30 minutes to 1 hour, until the fat has solidified. Remove the fat with a slotted spoon and discard. Line a sieve with a coffee filter and place it over a bowl. Strain the bourbon through the filter to remove the last of the fat. Transfer the flavored bourbon to a flask or bottle with a tight lid and store in the refrigerator.

USES ✻ While there are fans of the bacon manhattan, I think the best use of Bacon Bourbon is in a Bloody Mary, made simply with your favorite Bloody Mary mix. Serve it with a slice of crispy bacon and call it a Bloody Miss Piggy.

Old-Fashioned

The old-fashioned is one of my three favorite bourbon cocktails. (Or is that four favorites? No, better make it five.) But really, if I had to stick with only one cocktail for the rest of my life, this would be my choice. My husband's version is perfect.

MAKES 1 DRINK

¼ ounce simple syrup (page 22)
2 dashes bitters (preferably Angostura or Fee Brothers,
    old-fashioned, whiskey barrel–aged, or orange flavor)
¼ orange slice, unpeeled
1 maraschino cherry
2 ounces bourbon
2 ounces club soda, plain seltzer, or water

Place the simple syrup and bitters in an old-fashioned glass. Add the fruit and muddle slightly with the blunt end of a wooden muddler.

Fill the glass with ice. Add the bourbon and stir. Top with the club soda, seltzer, or water.

SIMPLE SYRUP

What happens when you stir granulated sugar into a cold mixture? You get a drink that looks like a snow globe, with a slurry of sugar at the bottom. The trick to making great sweetened beverages, from ice tea to cocktails, is to use sugar that's already dissolved into a liquid.

Simple syrup is a staple in my refrigerator. Not only do I use it in drinks, but I keep it around to jazz up fruit salad and to add a quick shot of flavor to plain seltzer, which I drink instead of soft drinks.

The amount of sugar in simple syrup varies depending on how thick you want the syrup, from a ratio of ¼ cup sugar to 1 cup water (great for hummingbird feeders) to a ratio of 1 cup sugar to 1 cup water. You can go higher, with more sugar than water, but the half-and-half mixture is the one I prefer for drinks.

It's even more fun to make flavored simple syrups, particularly mint syrup, which we keep on hand all summer. I also love ginger syrup, but the possibilities for flavors are endless.

Simple syrup: Combine 1 cup sugar and 1 cup water in a small saucepan. Bring to a simmer and stir until the sugar is dissolved and the water is clear. (You shouldn't feel any graininess of undissolved sugar at the bottom of the pan when you stir.) Remove from the heat. Cool briefly and refrigerate, preferably in a bottle with a spout. Keeps indefinitely.

Mint syrup: Make the simple syrup as directed, but when you remove the syrup from the heat, stir in 2 tightly packed cups of fresh mint leaves. Let stand for 30–45 minutes, or until cool. Strain the syrup and discard the mint leaves. Refrigerate the syrup as directed above. Keeps about 6 weeks.

Ginger syrup: Start with ½ pound fresh ginger. Trim away any dried-out areas where the root has been cut. (There's no reason to peel the ginger since you're going to strain the syrup, but if you really want to, the easiest way to peel it is with the edge of a spoon.) Using the large holes on a box grater, grate the ginger into a bowl. You should have about 2 cups of grated ginger and juice. Place the ginger and juice in a medium saucepan with 1 cup sugar and 1 cup water. Bring to a boil, stirring, and cook briefly, for less than a minute, until the sugar is dissolved. Remove from the heat and let stand for 1 hour. Strain into a bottle, discarding the solids. Cover and refrigerate for up to 3 weeks. (Some solids will settle out, so shake before using.)

Manhattan

The manhattan is an indispensable, classic bourbon cocktail. Although you can serve it on the rocks, it is classically served straight up in a cocktail glass. Tip: Keep your vermouth in the refrigerator to maintain the best quality.

MAKES 1 DRINK

½ ounce sweet vermouth
2 dashes Angostura bitters
2 ounces bourbon
1 maraschino cherry

Place the vermouth, bitters, and bourbon in a mixing glass or cocktail shaker with ice. Stir or shake well.

Strain into a chilled cocktail glass. Garnish with the cherry.

For a dry manhattan, use dry vermouth instead of sweet vermouth.

For a perfect manhattan, use ¼ ounce each of sweet and dry vermouth and rye instead of bourbon.

Classic Mint Julep

We could argue for hours over the proper way to make a julep—whether to bruise the mint, crush the ice, use sugar syrup or granulated sugar or sugar cubes. In fact, I think we should debate those points. Let's sit somewhere in the shade and discuss it while we enjoy several juleps my way, preferably in the silver cups passed down from my in-laws.

MAKES 1 DRINK

¼ ounce simple syrup (page 22)
4 fresh mint leaves
Crushed ice
2 ounces bourbon
1 ounce water (optional)
1 mint sprig

Add the simple syrup and mint leaves to a julep cup and muddle with the blunt end of a wooden muddler.

Fill the cup with crushed ice. Add the bourbon and stir until the outside of the cup is well frosted. Refill with crushed ice or add the water if desired.

Garnish with the mint sprig and serve with a short straw.

MUDDLE-FREE OPTION ❋ Omit the mint leaves and replace the simple syrup with mint syrup (page 23). This has the advantage of not getting bits of mint in your teeth.

Mint Julep Tea

I've never been in Louisville during the Kentucky Derby, but I've had the luck to attend—and give—plenty of Derby parties. There's one trouble with juleps, though: You can't make them very fast, and everyone wants a drink in hand before it's time to sing "My Old Kentucky Home." This is the solution, served in cups with sprigs of mint.

MAKES 1½ QUARTS, OR ABOUT 8 SERVINGS;
double it for a party

1 cup sugar

1 cup water

2 cups fresh mint leaves

3 cups strong brewed tea, cooled

¼ cup fresh lemon juice

1 cup bourbon

Mint sprigs

Combine the sugar and water in a small saucepan. Bring to a simmer, stirring until the sugar is dissolved. Remove from the heat, stir in the mint leaves, and let stand for 30 minutes.

Strain the mint syrup into a 2-quart pitcher. Stir in the tea, lemon juice, and bourbon and chill. This can be made up to 24 hours in advance, but the tannins in the tea get bitter after a day or so.

Serve over ice and garnish each glass with a mint sprig.

Bourbon & Burn

One of the great mixers with bourbon is Blenheim's ginger ale, particularly the very hot Old No. 5. Made in Dillon, South Carolina, it's available in scattered locations all over the South. Since it can be hard to find, I like this version, made with ginger syrup instead) for a similar lip-tingling heat.

MAKES 1 DRINK

2 ounces bourbon
½ ounce ginger syrup (page 23)
Club soda or plain seltzer

Fill a rocks or old-fashioned glass with ice. Add the bourbon and ginger syrup. Top with a splash of club soda or seltzer and stir gently before serving.

Sazerac

This is the official state cocktail of Louisiana, but it's not a moth-balled relic. In my experience, it's alive and well made at bars all over New Orleans. It seems wasteful to swirl and discard the absinthe, but it's necessary. That step and Peychaud's bitters are the keys to the right flavor.

MAKES 1 DRINK

¼ ounce simple syrup (page 22)

3 dashes Peychaud's bitters

1½ ounces rye or bourbon

¼ ounce absinthe (see Note below)

1 strip of lemon peel

Fill an old-fashioned glass with ice and set aside to chill.

In a second old-fashioned glass, add the simple syrup, bitters, and rye or bourbon, then stir. Discard the ice from the chilled glass and add the absinthe. Swirl the absinthe in the glass until the inside is fully coated, then discard the excess.

Transfer the bourbon mixture to the chilled glass. Garnish with the lemon peel.

NOTE ❋ Instead of absinthe, you can use another anise-flavored spirit, such as Pernod, Herbsaint, Absente, or green Chartreuse.

Rhythm & Soul

Mixologist Greg Best of Holeman & Finch in Atlanta is an evil cocktail genius, especially when it comes to doing new things with bourbon. After we met at a Southern Foodways Alliance symposium, he agreed to share a recipe for this book. Here's his description: "If the sophisticated rhythm of a well-stirred manhattan was in a street fight with the deep heady soul of a sazerac, we all know they'd make up later and fall in love. This drink would be their love child."

MAKES 1 DRINK

---

2 teaspoons Herbsaint

1½ ounces bourbon, preferably a small-batch bourbon such as Wathen's

½ ounce Carpano Antica Formula vermouth (a sweet and bitter Italian vermouth)

½ ounce Amaro Averna (a Sicilian liqueur)

4 dashes Angostura bitters

1 strip of lemon peel

Fill an old-fashioned glass with cracked ice and add the Herbsaint. Set aside while you make the rest of the drink.

Fill a mixing glass with ice and add the bourbon, Carpano Antica, Averna, and bitters. Stir.

Swirl the Herbsaint and ice around in the old-fashioned glass to coat the inside, then pour them out. Strain the contents of the mixing glass into the chilled glass. Garnish with the lemon peel.

WHAT DOES IT MEAN?

Angel's share: The whiskey that evaporates from barrels as it ages into bourbon.

Bootlegger: Someone who sells smuggled whiskey. The term came from the nickname for a flat bottle that could be tucked into a boot and refilled at a tavern.

Single-barrel bourbon: Bourbon bottled from one barrel. Usually 130 barrels are combined to make a batch, with water added to lower the proof.

Tailbox: A copper and glass box where white dog—unaged corn whiskey—is collected at the top of a column still.

Whiskey thief: A long copper tube that's used to draw samples from barrels of bourbon.

Seelbach Cocktail

I've had two life-changing experiences with cocktails. One was the first time I made a manhattan. The second was when I first saw this recipe. Bourbon and sparkling wine? It sounded disgusting. But after one sip, I was in love. The delicate rose color, the spicy flavor, and the mixture of bourbon and bubbles have made this a house favorite. Don't skimp and use only one kind of bitters. The combination of Peychaud's and Angostura is critical.

MAKES 1 DRINK

1 ounce bourbon

½ ounce Cointreau or Triple Sec

7 dashes Peychaud's bitters

7 dashes Angostura bitters

4 ounces chilled sparkling wine (Prosecco or Spanish cava work fine)

1 strip of orange peel

In this order, pour the bourbon, Cointreau, Peychaud's, Angostura, and sparkling wine into a champagne flute. Rub the orange peel around the rim of the glass and then drop it into drink.

Whiskey Sour

It sounds dated, but this drink is so refreshing. It deserves to stay in circulation.

MAKES 1 DRINK

---

1 ounce fresh lemon juice
½ ounce simple syrup (page 22)
2 ounces bourbon
¼ lemon slice
1 maraschino cherry

Combine the lemon juice, simple syrup, and bourbon in a cocktail shaker filled with ice. Shake until chilled. Strain into a sour glass (also known as a Delmonico glass). Garnish with the lemon and cherry.

NOTE ❋ Lemon juice can vary in tartness, so taste the drink before serving and add a little more simple syrup if needed.

John Collins

There's a whole family of Collinses, from the more familiar Tom Collins to the Irish whiskey–based Michael Collins. At heart, a Collins is really a sour with club soda added.

MAKES 1 DRINK

¾ ounce fresh lemon juice
1 ounce simple syrup (page 22)
2 ounces bourbon
2 ounces club soda
¼ lemon slice
1 maraschino cherry

Place the lemon juice, simple syrup, and bourbon in a tall, thin Collins glass and stir.

Fill with ice and top with the club soda. Garnish with the lemon and cherry.

Westfield Road Bourbon Slush

Westfield Road in Charlotte's historic Myers Park neighborhood is an unusually close-knit street where people get together for everything from trick-or-treating in the fall to tomato-tasting crawls in the summer. I'm lucky enough to know several residents, which is how I discovered Laura Yandell's bourbon slush, served at every gathering. The slush consistency is very cold and icy. Personally, I like to stir and poke it with a spoon as it melts. If you want to drink it more quickly, serve it with a splash of ginger ale.

MAKES 12–14 SERVINGS

---

4 regular-sized tea bags

2 cups boiling water

2 cups sugar

1 (12-ounce) can frozen orange juice concentrate, thawed

1 (12-ounce) can frozen lemonade concentrate, thawed

3 cups bourbon

7 cups cold water

Ginger ale (optional)

Add the tea bags to the boiling water and let stand for 3 minutes. Remove the tea bags and discard.

Pour the hot tea into a large bowl or plastic container (a plastic cake carrier works great). Stir in the sugar until dissolved. Stir in the juices, bourbon, and cold water.

Mix well and place in the freezer. Freeze until firm, 24–48 hours. Remove from the freezer 30 minutes before serving and stir well since the alcohol tends to settle on the bottom. If you want to serve it sooner, spoon it into wide glasses and serve it with a spoon, or top it with a splash of ginger ale.

Frozen Mint Julep

Bill Smith, chef of Crook's Corner in Chapel Hill, North Carolina, is the devious taste master behind this refreshing drink. He learned to make the mint sorbet from a pastry chef he once worked with. She could never keep the stuff around once the kitchen staff figured out how good it was with bourbon poured over it.

MAKES 3–4 CUPS MINT SORBET,
or enough for about 12 juleps

2 cups sugar
4 cups water
4 cups mint leaves
Zest of 2 lemons
2 cups fresh lemon juice (from about 9 lemons)
Bourbon

Mix the sugar and water in a nonreactive (nonaluminum) saucepan and bring to a boil. Boil for 5 minutes. Remove from the heat. Submerge the mint leaves and lemon zest in the liquid, cover, and steep for at least 15 minutes. (Don't boil after adding the mint leaves or it won't set up.)

Strain the liquid and chill. Freeze it in an ice cream freezer according to the manufacturer's directions.

To serve, place a small scoop of mint sorbet in a rocks glass and top it with a generous splash of bourbon. Serve with a small straw to drink the bourbon through the sorbet.

Hot Toddy

It may sound old-fashioned, but on a cold night, a toddy is a comforting thing, especially if you have a chest cold—or just think you feel one coming on.

MAKES 1 DRINK

---

2 ounces bourbon

4 ounces hot water

½ teaspoon light brown sugar

½ teaspoon honey

1 lemon slice

1 clove

1 cinnamon stick

Place the bourbon, hot water, brown sugar, and honey in a mug and stir until the sugar is dissolved.

Add the lemon slice, clove, and cinnamon stick and serve. (If it's not hot enough, microwave it for 30 seconds.)

Yes, Real Eggnog

You know it's almost Christmas when cartons of eggnog show up in the dairy case. (Given the ever-advancing Christmas shopping season, maybe it's just a sign that we've passed Labor Day.) If you really want to suck up to Santa, put real, from-scratch eggnog out with the cookies.

MAKES 4 SERVINGS

---

4 eggs, at room temperature
½ cup plus 1 tablespoon sugar, divided
2 cups whole milk
1 cup heavy cream
¼ cup bourbon
1 whole nutmeg

Separate the yolks and whites using the three-bowl method so you don't ruin a whole batch of whites with one broken yolk. Crack the first egg and catch the whites in one bowl, then place the yolk in a second bowl; pour the whites in a third bowl and then continue the process with the remaining eggs.

Place the yolks and ½ cup sugar in a mixing bowl and beat on high speed until the yolks are light and very pale yellow and a ribbon drips off the beaters when you raise them.

Lightly mix the milk, cream, and bourbon into the egg yolk mixture.

Using a second mixing bowl and clean beaters, beat the egg whites on slow speed until foamy. Increase the speed to high and add the remaining 1 tablespoon sugar, beating until the whites hold soft peaks that curve over when the beaters are lifted.

Using a rubber spatula, fold the egg whites into the cream mixture.

Serve immediately or chill for up to 1 hour. Top each serving with freshly grated nutmeg.

Appetizers

Cocktail hour is the time to sit, relax, and savor.
And a well-made cocktail deserves a nibble or nosh
to savor with it. Put together several noshes and
your cocktail hour becomes a cocktail party.

Bourbon–Chicken Liver Pâté

With its smooth texture and rich flavor, pâté raises chicken livers to a higher calling. In this version, a little bit of mayo makes it even smoother, while bacon gives a bit of extra texture.

MAKES ABOUT 4 CUPS

---

1 pound chicken livers (preferably from pasture-raised chickens)
6 slices bacon, diced
1 shallot, diced
½ cup plus 1 tablespoon bourbon, divided
1 cup heavy cream
2 tablespoons mayonnaise
2 tablespoons unsalted butter, at room temperature
2 teaspoons fresh thyme leaves
1 teaspoon kosher salt
1 teaspoon freshly ground black pepper
Crackers or baguette slices for serving

Rinse the livers and pat dry with a paper towel. Trim away any tough cartilage or veins.

Fry the bacon in a large skillet over medium-high heat until brown and just a little crisp. Remove from the skillet with a slotted spoon and drain on a paper towel.

Add the shallot to the hot bacon fat and stir. Lower the heat to medium and cook for 2–3 minutes, until starting to soften. Add the livers and cook for about 5 minutes, stirring occasionally, until brown on the outside but still a little pink on the inside.

Pour the livers and shallot into a food processor. Place the skillet back on the heat and add ⅓ cup bourbon. Bring to a boil, stirring up any browned bits. Add the cream, stir, and boil for 2–3 minutes until thickened. Pour into the food processor with the livers.

Process until smooth. Add the mayonnaise, butter, thyme, salt, and pepper. Process until smooth.

Stir in the bacon and the remaining 1 tablespoon bourbon.

Spread in several small crocks or ramekins and chill overnight. Serve with crackers or slices of baguette.

NOTE ❋ This can be made 2 days in advance and refrigerated. Or it can be wrapped tightly and frozen for up to 2 months.

Bourbon Dogs

These are hopelessly or charmingly retro, depending on your perspective. But take them to a party in a chafing dish or small slow cooker, and people will flip over them.

MAKES 6–8 SERVINGS,
or enough for a party with a bunch of other appetizers

---

1 (32-ounce) package smoked cocktail weinies
2 cups ketchup
¾ cup packed light brown sugar
¾ cup bourbon
1 tablespoon minced onion
½ cup water
Toothpicks for serving

Combine all the ingredients in a saucepan. Simmer for 25 minutes. (Or combine everything in an ovenproof baking dish and place in a 300° oven for 25–30 minutes.)

Place in a chafing dish or small slow cooker set on low. Serve with a slotted spoon and provide cocktail toothpicks.

Bourbon Pimento Cheese

The indispensable "pâté" of the South, pimento cheese takes all kinds of forms. Instead of the sandwich-spread version, this one is dressed up in party clothes to use as a spread or dip. You could also stuff celery sticks with it as an hors d'oeuvre.

MAKES 2 CUPS

---

2 cups shredded extra-sharp cheddar

4 tablespoons unsalted butter, at room temperature

3 tablespoons bourbon

1 (2-ounce) jar diced pimentos, drained

2 cloves garlic, minced

½ teaspoon Tabasco sauce

¼ teaspoon cayenne pepper

½ teaspoon salt

Crackers or celery sticks for serving

Combine the cheese, butter, and bourbon in a mixing bowl and beat with an electric mixer until it forms a paste. Beat in the pimentos, garlic, Tabasco, cayenne pepper, and salt.

Pack into a crock, cover, and chill until ready to use.

Serve with crackers or use to stuff celery sticks.

Bourbon Shrimp Paste

Shrimp paste is a spread made from puréed shrimp and butter, and it's wonderful on crackers or as a topping for hot grits. It led me to this recipe, which is even more wonderful.

MAKES 3 CUPS

---

1 pound raw shrimp, unpeeled (thawed if frozen)

½ cup bourbon

2 large cloves garlic

1 (8-ounce) package cream cheese, at room temperature

1 stick unsalted butter, at room temperature

1 teaspoon Worcestershire sauce

2 teaspoons Dijon mustard

½ teaspoon salt

Chopped parsley or Spanish smoked paprika

Crackers for serving

Bring a pot of salted water to a boil. Add the shrimp and cook for 3–4 minutes, until the shells are pink. Drain.

Place the bourbon in a heatproof bowl large enough to hold the shrimp. As soon as the shrimp are cool enough to handle but still quite warm, shell them and drop them into the bourbon, stirring to make sure they're submerged. Cool for 30 minutes.

Place the shrimp and bourbon in a food processor with the garlic and pulse until the shrimp are finely chopped. Add the cream cheese, butter, Worcestershire sauce, mustard, and salt. Process until combined.

Scrape into a crock and sprinkle the top with chopped parsley or paprika. Chill for several hours or overnight until firm. This can be refrigerated for up to 4 days.

Serve chilled with crackers.

NOTE ❋ You can divide the shrimp paste between several small bowls and freeze some for up to 2 months. Thaw it overnight in the refrigerator before serving.

Bleu-Bourbon Spread

There's so much more to blue cheese than just plain blue cheese. Cheeses like Gorgonzola and Stilton cost a little more, but they bring rich flavor to the table.

MAKES 1½ CUPS

½ cup chopped pecans
3 slices thick-cut bacon, diced
8 ounces good-quality blue cheese, such as Gorgonzola or
    Stilton
8 ounces shredded white cheddar
1 tablespoon unsalted butter, at room temperature
2 tablespoons bourbon
Crackers or baguette slices for serving

Spread the chopped pecans in a dry skillet over medium heat and toast, stirring, just until fragrant. Remove from the skillet and set aside to cool.

Fry the bacon in the skillet over medium heat, stirring often, until brown and just starting to crisp. Remove from the skillet and drain on a paper towel.

Crumble the blue cheese, then place in a mixing bowl with the cheddar and butter. Beat until smooth and well combined. Beat in the bourbon, then stir in the pecans and bacon.

Spread in a crock or small serving bowl and chill until firm. Serve with crackers or baguette slices.

Tipsy Jezebel Sauce

There's a lot of speculation about where Jezebel sauce got its name—whether the mixture of sweet and hot reminded people of a saucy woman's behavior or whether the name was inspired by Bette Davis's sweet and hot character in the movie Jezebel. *Either way, I always thought a sauce named for a southern woman's nature ought to have a touch of spirit, too.*

MAKES ABOUT 2½ CUPS

1 (12-ounce) jar pineapple preserves
1 cup apple jelly
½ cup apricot preserves
2 tablespoons prepared horseradish (see Note below)
2 tablespoons Dijon mustard
3 tablespoons bourbon

Whisk together all the ingredients. Refrigerate until ready to use. It will keep for weeks.

Serve over cream cheese spread on crackers, or use to glaze a pork loin or pork tenderloin. Or spread with mayonnaise on a turkey sandwich. It also goes great with brie. If you want, put it in small jars to give as gifts.

NOTE ❋ Prepared horseradish is usually found in a store's refrigerated section near the cream cheese. It loses potency after it's opened, so if you have a jar that's been open for a few months, it's better to buy a new one.

Rebecca Sauce with Strawberries

The original version of this dessert sauce is usually credited to the Galt House Hotel in Louisville, Kentucky, but it was made with sour cream instead of confectioners' sugar. I make a simpler version for Derby parties. I have a serving platter with three sections just for this. Be careful—it can sneak up on you.

MAKES 6–8 SERVINGS

---

2 cups confectioners' sugar, plus more for serving
2 tablespoons bourbon
1 teaspoon vanilla
About 1 tablespoon heavy cream
Fresh, ripe strawberries, stems on

Mix together the confectioners' sugar, bourbon, vanilla, and cream.

Serve the dip in a bowl surrounded by strawberries along with a small dish of confectioners' sugar. Dip a strawberry in the bourbon mixture, then into confectioners' sugar.

Main Dishes and Sides

Bourbon can play so many roles in the kitchen, from deglazing a pan to boosting flavor. It adds a spicy note to hearty winter dishes and a special touch to summery grilled recipes. Heating bourbon can reduce its flavor, so in many dishes, I add it twice: once in cooking and again at the end.

Bourbon Benedict

Save this one for a special morning at home. I use bacon glazed with brown sugar and bourbon and a bourbon-flavored hollandaise. In my experience, the alcohol makes a traditional hollandaise more prone to curdling. So I reached back to the 1970s for a microwave version that not only is more forgiving but can be made in advance, refrigerated, and reheated when you need it.

MAKES 4 SERVINGS

1 tablespoon packed light brown sugar

5 tablespoons bourbon, divided

4 slices thick-cut bacon

4 tablespoons unsalted butter

2 egg yolks

2 teaspoons fresh lemon juice

¼ cup heavy cream

1 teaspoon Dijon mustard

Salt to taste

4 eggs

2 English muffins

Combine the brown sugar and 3 tablespoons bourbon in a small bowl or pie plate. Add the bacon and turn to coat. Let stand for 30 minutes.

Preheat the oven to 350°. Line a rimmed baking sheet with foil. Remove the bacon from the bourbon mixture and lay the strips on the foil, leaving a little room between the strips. Bake for 20–30 minutes, until browned but not too crisp. Remove from the oven.

Place the butter in a microwave-safe bowl. Microwave on high for 30 seconds. Remove from the microwave and stir. If the butter isn't melted, microwave it for 30 seconds again. Remove it from the microwave and let it stand a few minutes.

Whisk in the egg yolks, lemon juice, and cream. Return to the microwave and cook on high for 1 minute, whisking every 20 seconds. Remove from the microwave and whisk in the mustard and the remaining 2 tablespoons bourbon. Add salt if needed. The sauce can be set aside for up to 1 hour or refrigerated overnight.

Add about 1½ inches of water to a heavy skillet and bring to a boil. Reduce the heat to maintain a slow simmer. Carefully crack each egg into the water, swirling the water a little to bring the whites toward the yolk to create a compact shape. Cook until the whites are set but the yolks are still soft. Turn off the heat.

Toast the muffin halves. Microwave the hollandaise for 30 seconds to rewarm it if needed. (If it's refrigerated, you may need to microwave it for 1 minute.)

Place a muffin half on a small plate and add about 1 table-spoon hollandaise. Cut 1 slice of bacon into 2 pieces and place the pieces on the muffin half. Remove a poached egg from the hot water with a slotted spoon and pat it dry around the edges with a paper towel. Place it on the bacon, then ladle more of the hollandaise over the top.

Repeat with the remaining bacon, muffin halves, and poached eggs. Serve immediately.

Bourbon Chicken Stroganoff

Beef might be traditional, but this version, with big chunks of chicken and mushrooms, is a hearty dinner on a cold night.

MAKES 6 SERVINGS

1½ pounds boneless, skinless chicken thighs, trimmed of fat
    and cut into bite-sized pieces
½ teaspoon salt, plus more to taste
½ teaspoon freshly ground black pepper, plus more to taste
1½ teaspoons Spanish smoked paprika, divided
3 tablespoons olive oil, divided
8 ounces white mushrooms, quartered
1 shallot, minced, divided
2 teaspoons minced fresh thyme leaves, divided
4 cloves garlic, chopped
1 whole roasted red pepper from a jar, diced
½ cup bourbon
1 plum tomato, grated, skin discarded
½ cup sour cream
Egg noodles for serving, cooked according to package
    directions

Toss the chicken with the salt and pepper and ½ teaspoon paprika.

Heat 1 tablespoon olive oil in a nonstick skillet over medium-high heat. Add the mushrooms and cook for 2 minutes, until browned in spots. Add half the shallot and half the thyme and stir. Cook for 3–5 minutes. Remove from the skillet with a slotted spoon and place in a bowl.

With the skillet over medium heat, add 2 tablespoons oil. Add the chicken, garlic, remaining thyme and shallot, and 1 teaspoon paprika. Cook for 5–6 minutes, stirring often. Return the cooked mushrooms to the skillet and add the red pepper and bourbon. Bring to a boil for 2 minutes to reduce the bourbon slightly.

Reduce the heat to medium-low and stir in the tomato. Cover and simmer for about 10 minutes.

Stir in the sour cream and cook until just heated through. Taste and add more salt and pepper if needed.

Serve over hot buttered egg noodles.

COOKING WITH ALCOHOL

Alcohol is reduced during cooking, but it doesn't disappear completely. According to the U.S. Department of Agriculture, if you add alcohol to a boiling liquid and remove it from the heat, it loses 15 percent of the alcohol. If you flame alcohol in a pan, such as flambéing a dish, you lose 25 percent of the alcohol. If you add alcohol to a baked or simmered mixture, it retains less alcohol the longer it's cooked:

15 minutes: 40 percent
30 minutes: 35 percent
1 hour: 25 percent
1½ hours: 20 percent
2 hours: 10 percent
2½ hours: 5 percent

Beer and Bourbon Beef Stew

This dish is like bringing Irish stew to the South—just the thing for a chilly fall night.

MAKES 6 SERVINGS

4 slices bacon, chopped
1 large onion, diced
4–6 tablespoons unsalted butter, divided
8 ounces mushrooms, quartered
1/4 cup all-purpose flour
1/2 teaspoon salt
1/2 teaspoon freshly ground black pepper
2 pounds chuck roast, cut into 1-inch pieces
1/2 cup bourbon, divided
2 cups beef broth
1/2 cup Dijon mustard
1/2 cup dark beer, such as a stout
4 large carrots, halved lengthwise and sliced into half-moons
Pappardelle pasta or egg noodles for serving, cooked
    according to package directions

Fry the bacon in a 4- to 6-quart pot or Dutch oven until it begins to crisp. Remove with a slotted spoon and drain on a paper towel.

Add the onion to the rendered fat in the pot and cook over medium heat until softened, about 10 minutes, reducing the heat if needed to keep it from getting too brown.

Add 2 tablespoons butter to the pot, then add the mushrooms, cooking and stirring frequently for about 5 minutes until browned in spots. Remove the onion and mushrooms with a slotted spoon and place in a bowl.

Combine the flour, salt, and pepper in a shallow bowl or on a wide plate. Working in several batches, toss some of the beef in the flour and shake off the excess. Add 2 tablespoons butter to the drippings in the pot over medium heat and add the floured beef, turning the pieces to brown them all over. Remove with a slotted spoon. Repeat with the remaining beef.

When all the beef is browned, remove the pot from the heat and immediately add the bourbon, stirring up the browned bits from the bottom. Return the pot to medium heat and stir in the broth and mustard.

Stir in the bacon, onion and mushrooms, and beef. Bring to a boil, then cover, reduce the heat to maintain a low simmer, and cook for 1½ hours, until the beef is very tender. Uncover, stir in the beer and carrots, and cook for 30 minutes.

Serve over hot buttered pappardelle pasta or egg noodles.

Pork Tenderloin with Mango-Bourbon Sauce

You can replace the mango with peaches if you prefer.

MAKES 6 SERVINGS

---

1 package pork tenderloins, about 1½ pounds (not marinated)
3–4 tablespoons barbecue dry rub (see Note below)
3 tablespoons olive oil, divided
¼ cup minced red onion
1½ cups diced mango (about 1 medium ripe mango;
    if using peaches instead, use 4–6)
¼ teaspoon salt
½ teaspoon ground coriander
¼ teaspoon cayenne pepper
2 tablespoons bourbon

Rinse the two tenderloins, then pat dry with a paper towel. Sprinkle each well with the dry rub. Lay the tapered tenderloins next to each other with the large end of one next to the small end of the other. Use several pieces of kitchen string (preferably cotton) to tie them together.

Wrap in plastic wrap and refrigerate for at least 1 hour or overnight. Remove from the refrigerator 30 minutes before cooking.

Preheat the oven to 375°. Place an ovenproof skillet, preferably nonstick, on the stove over medium-high heat. Add 2 tablespoons olive oil. Place the tied pork tenderloins in the skillet and cook for about 10 minutes, turning with tongs, until browned on all sides. Place the skillet in the oven and roast the tenderloins for about 30 minutes, until a meat thermometer reaches 150°.

Meanwhile, make the sauce. Heat the remaining 1 tablespoon olive oil in a pan over medium heat. Add the red onion and cook for about 5 minutes, stirring often, until it softens but still has some crunch. Stir in the mango, reduce the heat to medium-low, cover, and cook for about 5 minutes, until the mango is soft and juicy. Stir in the salt, coriander, and cayenne pepper. Remove from the heat and stir in the bourbon. The sauce can be made about 30 minutes before serving. Rewarm it over low heat before serving.

When the tenderloins are done, remove them from the oven and let stand for 5 minutes. Remove the string and slice the tenderloins into ½-inch rounds. Serve with Mango-Bourbon Sauce.

NOTE ✳ You can use a prepared dry rub or make your own by combining in a resealable container 1½ tablespoons sweet paprika, 1½ teaspoons Spanish smoked paprika, 1 tablespoon kosher salt, 1 tablespoon sugar, 1½ teaspoons dry mustard, 1 tablespoon chili powder, 1 tablespoon ground cumin, 1½ teaspoons freshly ground black pepper, 1 tablespoon garlic powder, 1 teaspoon cayenne pepper, 1 teaspoon celery salt, and 1½ teaspoons onion powder. Store at room temperature for up to several months. Makes ¾ cup.

Bourbon-Ginger Grilled
Pork Tenderloin

My friend Genna Hurley teaches water aerobics at our local YMCA. It's a great class because she keeps us moving for an hour—and because she lets us talk about food the whole time. Class motto: We eat, therefore we work out. She also shares her own recipes, including this easy grilled dish, perfect for a summer dinner.

MAKES 6 SERVINGS

1 package pork tenderloins, about 1½ pounds (not marinated)

¼ cup soy sauce

½ cup bourbon

2 tablespoons packed light brown sugar

3 cloves garlic, sliced

2 tablespoons diced ginger

2 teaspoons Worcestershire sauce

Rinse the two tenderloins and pat dry with a paper towel. Place in a resealable 1-gallon plastic bag.

Whisk together the soy sauce, bourbon, brown sugar, garlic, ginger, and Worcestershire sauce in a small bowl. Pour into the bag with the pork. Seal the bag, rotate it several times to distribute the marinade, and refrigerate for 8 hours or overnight. (If you're cooking on a work night, you can put this together in the morning and refrigerate it all day.)

Preheat a gas grill or light some charcoal and heat it until covered with white ash, then spread the coals on one side of the grill.

Remove the pork from the marinade. Place the two pieces of meat together, matching the narrow end of one to the wide end of the other to create a uniform size, then tie them together in several places with kitchen string. (You can skip this step if you prefer, but the meat will cook more evenly if the tenderloins are tied together.)

Place the meat directly over the coals or gas jets. Cover the grill and cook for 5 minutes.

Using tongs, roll the meat over a quarter turn and continue cooking, covered. Continue cooking, turning every 5 minutes or so, until browned on all sides. Move to the cooler side of the grill and cook for 10–15 minutes, until the interior registers 160° on a meat thermometer.

Remove from the heat and let stand for 5 minutes. Remove the string and slice into rounds to serve.

Bourbon-Glazed Salmon

The season for wild salmon is short, so I always feel like I have to make the best of it. Luckily, pretty good frozen wild salmon is available all year.

MAKES 4 SERVINGS

Nonstick cooking spray
2 tablespoons Dijon mustard
2 tablespoons bourbon
1 tablespoon maple syrup (preferably Grade B)
½ teaspoon Spanish smoked paprika
¼ teaspoon salt
1½–2 pounds skin-on wild salmon fillet

Preheat the oven to 450°. Spray a baking sheet with cooking spray.

Whisk together the mustard, bourbon, maple syrup, paprika, and salt in a small bowl. Place the salmon, skin-side down, on the prepared baking sheet. Pour the glaze over the fish and brush it to coat the top completely.

Roast until just cooked through, 8–10 minutes, then set the oven to broil and broil for 2–3 minutes, watching carefully to make sure the glaze doesn't burn.

Cut into 4 portions and serve.

Bourbon-Marinated Flank Steak

Grilling a flank steak is the perfect Saturday night dinner because it's easy and, if you're lucky, you'll end up with leftovers for stroganoff or a main-dish salad later in the week. A hint of bourbon adds sophistication to this easy East-meets-South steak marinade.

MAKES 4–6 SERVINGS

¼ cup hoisin sauce

1 tablespoon honey

1 teaspoon cayenne pepper

2 cloves garlic, minced

2 tablespoons bourbon

1 (1½- to 2-pound) flank steak

Whisk together the hoisin sauce, honey, cayenne pepper, garlic, and bourbon in a small bowl. Place the flank steak in a glass baking dish large enough to hold it in a single layer or in a large, resealable freezer bag. Add the marinade and turn the steak over several times to coat it.

Cover if using a glass dish and refrigerate for at least 2 hours or marinate at room temperature for no more than 1 hour.

Heat a gas grill or prepare a charcoal fire for direct grilling. Remove the flank steak from the marinade and grill for 10–15 minutes per side, depending on thickness (when you poke the thickest part with your finger, it should feel like it's beginning to get firm).

Remove from the grill and let stand for 10 minutes. Slice the steak diagonally across the grain and serve.

Spicy Bourbon Chicken Thighs

You can use chicken breasts if you prefer, but chicken thighs are richer and meatier—a great match for the bourbon-touched sauce.

MAKES 4 SERVINGS

---

2 teaspoons garlic powder

2 teaspoons chili powder

1 teaspoon salt

1 teaspoon ground cumin

1 teaspoon Spanish smoked paprika

½ teaspoon cayenne pepper

8 skin-on, bone-in chicken thighs

Nonstick cooking spray

4 tablespoons honey

3 tablespoons bourbon

2 teaspoons cider vinegar

Place an oven rack in the center position. Preheat the oven to 500°, then set it to broil.

Combine the garlic powder, chili powder, salt, cumin, paprika, and cayenne pepper in a mixing bowl. Add the chicken thighs and toss to coat.

Spray a broiler pan with cooking spray. Place the thighs on the pan skin-side down. Broil for 8 minutes. Turn and continue broiling for 6–8 minutes, until the juices run clear.

Whisk together the honey, bourbon, and vinegar in a small bowl. Remove the chicken from the broiler and brush with the bourbon glaze. Broil for 1 minute. Turn the thighs over, brush with the glaze, and broil for 1 minute. Turn skin-side up, brush again, and continue broiling until browned and well glazed.

Serve hot.

Honey-Bourbon Chicken Wings

Broiling turns out crispy wings without the mess and fat of deep-frying. Once you brush the wings with the honey-bourbon glaze, turn them often and watch them carefully so they don't burn.

MAKES 4 SERVINGS

---

4 pounds chicken wings, cut into flappers and drummettes
1/4 cup olive oil
Salt and freshly ground black pepper
1/4 cup plain rice vinegar
1 teaspoon crushed red pepper flakes
3/4 cup honey
2 tablespoons bourbon

Toss the chicken wings with the oil and season with salt and pepper. Place the wings, skin-side down, in a single layer on a rack over a broiler pan. You can place them close together, but leave a little space between each. Use a second pan and rack if you have to.

Place an oven rack in the center position and set the oven to broil. Place the wings under the broiler. Broil for 20 minutes, remove the pan from the oven, turn the wings, and place them back under the broiler for 15 minutes.

While the wings are broiling, combine the vinegar, red pepper flakes, and honey in a small saucepan. Heat just to a simmer for 1 minute and remove from the heat. Stir in the bourbon.

Brush the honey-bourbon glaze on both sides of wings. Return them to the oven and broil for 5 minutes. Brush the wings again on both sides, turn them, and broil for 5 minutes longer. Remove from the oven and brush again with the remaining glaze. Serve hot.

Bourbon Baked Beans

Making baked beans from scratch takes a while, but during most of that time, the beans are untended. You could use canned beans, but dried beans aren't that much more work and they'll keep their shape better over the long cooking time.

MAKES 8 SERVINGS

1 (16-ounce) bag dried navy or cannellini beans

4 onions, chopped, divided

4–5 slices bacon

¼ cup cider vinegar

2 (6-ounce) cans tomato paste

1 cup molasses

¾ cup bourbon, divided

1 teaspoon Worcestershire sauce

1 teaspoon dry mustard

½ teaspoon ground cumin

2 cloves garlic, smashed

1 teaspoon salt, plus more to taste

Rinse the beans and remove any stones or debris. Place in a heavy pot and cover with water. Bring to a boil, cover, remove from the heat, and let stand for at least 1 hour. (Or cover with water and soak overnight.)

Drain the beans and cover again with fresh water. Add half of the onions and the bacon. Bring to a boil over medium heat, reduce the heat, cover, and simmer for 45 minutes or until the beans are tender, adding more water if needed.

When the beans are tender, drain them, saving the cooking water.

Preheat the oven to 325°. Place the beans in a 2-quart baking dish with the vinegar, tomato paste, molasses, remaining onions, ½ cup bourbon, Worcestershire sauce, dry mustard, cumin, garlic, and salt. Mix well, cover, and bake for 2 hours.

Uncover and stir in the remaining ¼ cup bourbon. Stir in some of the cooking water if the beans look dry. Bake, uncovered, for 30 minutes longer.

NOTE ❧ If you'll be reheating the beans several times to serve them, refrigerate the bean-cooking water and add a little more as needed to keep the beans from getting dry.

Bourbon-Glazed Carrots

Cooking carrots with a glaze elevates them to a sophisticated side dish.

MAKES 4 SERVINGS

1 pound carrots, sliced into ½-inch rounds
3 tablespoons honey
2 tablespoons bourbon
1 tablespoon balsamic vinegar
1 teaspoon salt

Place the carrots in a large nonstick skillet and cover with water. Cover and bring to a boil over medium-high heat. Reduce the heat to medium and simmer for 8 minutes or until crisp-tender. Drain.

Place the carrots back in the skillet and add the honey, bourbon, balsamic vinegar, and salt. Cook over medium-high heat, stirring occasionally, for 5 minutes, until the carrots are coated with the glaze.

Remove from the heat and serve hot.

Bourbon-Pecan Sweet Potatoes

The ideal Thanksgiving dinner has family members of all ages around the table. But sometimes the family is just adults, and an adult dish is right at home.

MAKES 6 SERVINGS

3 medium sweet potatoes
4 tablespoons unsalted butter, plus 1 tablespoon melted unsalted butter, divided
¼ cup orange juice
½ cup packed light brown sugar
3 tablespoons bourbon
½ teaspoon salt
½ teaspoon cinnamon
¼ teaspoon nutmeg
1 cup chopped pecans

Peel the sweet potatoes, cut them into chunks, and place them in a saucepan. Cover with water, bring to a boil, reduce the heat, and simmer for about 30 minutes, until fork-tender. (Or bake the scrubbed, unpeeled sweet potatoes in a 350° oven until soft, about 40 minutes. Let stand until cool enough to handle, then remove the skins and continue as directed.)

Preheat the oven to 350°. Place the hot, cooked sweet potatoes in a mixing bowl and beat in 4 tablespoons butter and the orange juice, brown sugar, bourbon, salt, cinnamon, and nutmeg.

Place in a 1½-quart baking dish. Top with the pecans and drizzle with 1 tablespoon melted butter. Bake for 20–30 minutes, until hot. (If the pecans begin to get too brown, tent loosely with foil.)

Serve hot.

Bourbon Peaches

My good friend Andrea Weigl is a food writer and a home canner who sends me jars of tasty things every Christmas. She suggested this variation on the more traditional brandied peaches. They're sweet, but they make a beautiful side dish for roast pork or a Thanksgiving table.

MAKES 2 QUARTS

Juice of 1 lemon or 1 teaspoon Fruit Fresh
3 pounds small, ripe peaches (about 10–12)
5 cups sugar
5 cups water
About 2 cups bourbon

Bring a small pot of water to a boil and fill a bowl with ice water and either the lemon juice or Fruit Fresh.

Place the peaches in the boiling water for 1–2 minutes. Immediately remove with a slotted spoon and drop in the ice water. Remove and discard the peach skins and return the peaches to the ice water while you make the syrup.

Combine the sugar and water in a large pot over medium heat. Stir until the sugar is dissolved. Add the peaches and cook until they're tender enough to pierce with a skewer, about 15 minutes.

Remove the peaches to a bowl and continue cooking the syrup until it reaches 220–222°. Sterilize 2 quart jars and keep hot. Pack the whole peaches into the jars. Fill the jars two-thirds of the way up with syrup, then the rest of the way with bourbon, leaving ½ inch of headspace. Wipe the rims with a clean towel, place the lids on the jars, and screw the rings on tightly.

Process for 15 minutes on a rack in a hot water bath. Remove, cool, and tap the jars to make sure they're sealed. (If they're not sealed, they'll make a tinny sound when you tap them and the center won't be depressed.) Store in a cool, dark place for 6 months before opening. Or skip the water bath, refrigerate, and use within a month.

Bourbon Barbecue Sauce

The combination of molasses and bourbon adds a smoky depth to a basic sauce that's perfect for glazing ribs or using as a dip for anything from pork butt to chicken to brisket.

MAKES 1½ CUPS

2 tablespoons unsalted butter

1 tablespoon vegetable oil

1 onion, diced

¼ cup plus 2 tablespoons bourbon, divided

2 cups ketchup

¼ cup molasses (or sorghum or dark cane syrup)

½ cup packed light brown sugar

1 tablespoon garlic powder

1 tablespoon dry mustard

2 tablespoons apple cider vinegar

1 teaspoon salt

½ teaspoon freshly ground black pepper

Heat the butter and oil in a medium saucepan over medium heat until the butter is melted. Add the onion and sauté slowly for 10 minutes, until softened and translucent, adjusting the heat if needed to keep it from scorching.

Add 2 tablespoons bourbon, stir, and bring to a boil. Cook for 1–2 minutes, until the bourbon has almost evaporated.

Add the ketchup, molasses, brown sugar, garlic powder, dry mustard, vinegar, salt, and pepper and stir. Bring to a simmer, reduce the heat to medium-low, and cook for 20 minutes, stirring often so it doesn't stick as it reduces.

Remove from the heat and stir in the remaining ¼ cup bourbon. Cool and refrigerate until ready to use.

Desserts and Other Sweet Things

With flavor notes that include caramel and vanilla, is it any wonder that bourbon is good in so many sweets? There are classics, from bourbon balls to Lane Cake, and new creations, such as Bourbon Cream Topping thickened with mascarpone and Bourbon-Coffee Brûlée. Bourbon even gives butterscotch concoctions real pizzazz.

Chocolate-Nut Bourbon Balls

Label these "adults only" when you add them to a Christmas cookie stash. If you have trouble finding chocolate wafer cookies, look on the aisle with the ice cream toppings.

MAKES ABOUT 5 DOZEN

1½ cups pecans, divided

1 (9-ounce) package chocolate wafer cookies

½ cup plus 1 tablespoon confectioners' sugar, divided

½ teaspoon instant espresso powder

⅓ cup bourbon

3 tablespoons dark corn syrup

⅔ cup semisweet chocolate chips, melted

Spread the pecans in a dry skillet over medium heat. Cook, stirring often, until the pecans are lightly toasted and fragrant. Cool.

Grind the cookies in a food processor to make 2 cups of fine crumbs. Place in a mixing bowl.

Without cleaning out the food processor, chop 1 cup pecans and ½ cup confectioners' sugar. Add to the cookie crumbs.

Dissolve the espresso powder in the bourbon. Stir into the crumbs with the corn syrup and chocolate. Mix until completely moistened.

Place the remaining ½ cup pecans and 1 tablespoon confectioners' sugar in the food processor and pulse until finely ground. Place in a bowl.

Line a baking sheet with wax paper.

Pinch off bits of dough and roll into 1-inch balls. Toss each one in the pecan-sugar mixture to coat and place on the prepared baking sheet. Chill until firm.

Place in an airtight container between layers of waxed paper. Store in the refrigerator for up to 3 days or in the freezer for up to 2 months.

Pecan Bourbon Balls

Take out the chocolate (well, most of the chocolate) and keep the pecans and you've got another variation on bourbon balls to welcome a winter holiday.

MAKES ABOUT 4 DOZEN

1½ cups pecans, divided

1 cup plus 2 tablespoons confectioners' sugar, divided

1 (12-ounce) box vanilla wafers

2 tablespoons unsweetened cocoa

½ cup bourbon

¼ cup light corn syrup

¼ teaspoon salt

Spread the pecans in a dry skillet over medium heat. Cook, stirring often, until the pecans are lightly toasted and fragrant. Cool.

Place ½ cup pecans and 2 tablespoons confectioners' sugar in a food processor. Pulse until finely ground. Place in a bowl.

Place the remaining 1 cup pecans and the vanilla wafers in the food processor. Pulse until finely ground. Add the remaining 1 cup confectioners' sugar, cocoa, bourbon, corn syrup, and salt. Process until well combined.

Pinch off bits of dough and roll into 1-inch balls. Toss each ball in the pecan-sugar mixture. Place the balls on a baking sheet. Refrigerate for 2–3 hours, until firm.

Store in an airtight container in the refrigerator for up to 1 week or in the freezer for up to 2 months.

WHICH WHISKEY IS WHICH?

First, what's the difference between whiskey and whisky? "Whisky" is the preferred spelling in Scotland and Canada. Elsewhere, bourbon, rye, and Irish whiskey are all "whiskeys." If there's no indication of origin, the generic term is usually "whiskey."

Bourbon: Whiskey that meets a list of criteria, including being made in America, being aged in charred new American oak barrels for at least two years, containing at least 51 percent corn, with additional wheat and barley, and being distilled to no more than 80 percent alcohol, put into the barrel at no more than 62.5 percent alcohol, and bottled at a minimum of 40 percent alcohol.

Rye: Whiskey labeled as rye must include at least 51 percent rye in the mash.

Scotch: A malt or grain whiskey. Different types include single malt or blended malt.

Tennessee whiskey: Bourbon made in Tennessee, usually (but not always) with the added step of filtering the liquor through maple charcoal before barreling, called the Lincoln County process. Jack Daniels and George Dickel are both Tennessee whiskeys.

Canadian whisky: A blended whiskey made from multiple grains and corn. "Rye whiskey" and "Canadian whisky" are interchangeable terms, even though most Canadian whisky now contains little or no rye.

Orange-Coconut Bourbon Balls

This is a rare version of bourbon balls that doesn't include nuts. So people with nut allergies can join in the fun.

MAKES ABOUT 4 DOZEN

1½ cups frozen grated coconut, thawed, divided

1 (12-ounce) box vanilla wafers

1 cup confectioners' sugar

¼ cup bourbon

¼ cup light corn syrup

2 tablespoons orange liqueur, such as Grand Marnier or
   Triple Sec

Place 1 cup coconut and the vanilla wafers in a food processor. Process until well ground. Add the confectioners' sugar, bourbon, corn syrup, and orange liqueur. Process until a dough forms.

Pinch off bits of dough and roll into 1-inch balls. Roll the balls in the remaining ½ cup coconut. Place the balls on a baking sheet and refrigerate until firm.

Store in an airtight container in the refrigerator for up to a week or in the freezer for up to 2 months.

Kentucky Colonels

While most bourbon balls are a cross between a cookie and a cake, these are definitely candies. Many bourbon distilleries serve a version in their tasting rooms (and sell them in their gift shops, of course), although those are usually made with a pecan half on top instead of chopped pecans inside. I prefer them this way. The pecans add texture to balance the super-sweet filling.

MAKES ABOUT 3 DOZEN

1 stick unsalted butter, at room temperature
3½ cups confectioners' sugar
6 tablespoons bourbon
¼ teaspoon salt
½ teaspoon vanilla
¼ cup minced pecans
8 (1-ounce) squares semisweet chocolate
2 teaspoons shortening

Combine the butter and confectioners' sugar in a mixing bowl and beat with an electric mixer until smooth. (It will look fluffy, like canned white frosting.) Beat in the bourbon, salt, and vanilla. Stir in the pecans.

Refrigerate the mixture for 1 hour, until firm enough to handle. Working quickly so the warmth of your hands doesn't soften the mixture, pinch off small pieces and roll into 1-inch balls, then place on a baking sheet lined with wax paper. Place in the freezer for several hours or overnight.

Chop the chocolate into small pieces and place in a small saucepan over medium-low heat. Stir often until completely melted. Stir in the shortening and remove from the heat.

Remove the pecan balls from the freezer, and, using a fork, drop each ball into the chocolate, turn to coat, then scoop it up with the fork and let the excess chocolate drip off before returning it to the baking sheet. When all the balls are coated, place in the refrigerator until the chocolate is set. Store in an airtight container in the refrigerator or the freezer.

Salted Bourbon Caramels

These caramels have the perfect texture—creamy and just a little chewy without threatening to take out your fillings. Be patient when you use the candy thermometer. When you attach it to the side of the pan, make sure the tip isn't touching the bottom, and watch it carefully. It can seem like the temperature isn't going up, and then it will suddenly jump. That's the nature of hot sugar.

MAKES ABOUT 30 PIECES

---

2 sticks unsalted butter, plus about 1 tablespoon for the pan

2 cups granulated sugar

1 cup packed light brown sugar

1 cup milk (nonfat or 2 percent)

1 cup heavy cream

1 cup light corn syrup

1 teaspoon vanilla

½ teaspoon salt

2 tablespoons bourbon

1–2 teaspoons flaky sea salt

Line a 13 × 9-inch pan with foil and butter the foil. (The easiest way to line a pan with foil without tearing it is to turn the pan over, press the foil over the bottom to shape it, then turn the pan right-side up and drop the foil into it.)

Combine the remaining 2 sticks butter and the sugars, milk, cream, and corn syrup in a 4- to 5-quart saucepan. Place over medium heat, stirring occasionally, until the butter is melted and the sugar is dissolved and the mixture reaches a full boil, 15–20 minutes. (Don't be tempted to hurry it by cranking up the heat—you may burn it.)

Attach a candy thermometer to the side of the pan, adjusting it so the first couple of inches of the thermometer are immersed but the tip isn't touching the bottom of the pan. Cook for 25–30 minutes, stirring occasionally and lowering the heat if it starts to darken, until the mixture reaches 244°.

Remove from the heat and immediately stir in the vanilla, ½ teaspoon salt, and bourbon. Pour into the prepared pan. Let stand for 5 minutes, then sprinkle with the sea salt.

Let stand for 1–2 hours, until completely cool. Refrigerate until firm, then remove from the pan by lifting out the foil and cut into 2 × 1-inch pieces. Place in an airtight container with wax paper between the layers or wrap each candy in wax paper. Store in the refrigerator.

Butter-Bourbon Pudding

There's no scotch in butterscotch, but bourbon tastes better anyway in this very old-fashioned version of the classic. Needless to say, it's no longer nursery food. This is why you go to the trouble to grow up.

MAKES 4–6 SERVINGS

¾ cup packed light brown sugar

2 tablespoons cornstarch

¼ teaspoon salt

1½ cups milk (nonfat or 2 percent)

½ cup heavy cream

3 egg yolks

2 tablespoons unsalted butter, cut into pieces,
   at room temperature

2 tablespoons bourbon

1 teaspoon vanilla

Flaky sea salt (optional)

In a heavy 1½- to 2-quart saucepan, whisk together the brown sugar, cornstarch, and ¼ teaspoon salt until mixed. (Don't worry if there are a few lumps; they'll cook out.) Whisk in the milk and cream. Cook over medium heat, whisking frequently, until bubbly and starting to thicken, about 10 minutes. Cook, stirring, 2 minutes longer, then remove from the heat.

Beat the egg yolks in a small, heatproof bowl. Add a few tablespoons of the hot milk mixture, whisking thoroughly, then slowly pour the yolks into the hot milk mixture in the saucepan and stir.

Return to medium heat and cook for 2 minutes, stirring constantly, until thickened. Remove from the heat and whisk in the butter a little at a time, until melted. Then stir in the bourbon and vanilla.

Pour into 4–6 parfait glasses, ramekins, or small bowls. Serve warm or cover with plastic wrap and refrigerate until ready to serve. (Press the wrap onto the surface of the pudding if you don't like pudding skin.) Sprinkle with sea salt before serving, if desired.

Bourbon-Coffee Brûlée

What is it about coffee and bourbon? The flavors complement each other, making a great dessert to end a dinner party.

MAKES 6 SERVINGS

2½ cups heavy cream
1 teaspoon instant espresso powder
9 egg yolks
¾ cup sugar
6 tablespoons bourbon
1 teaspoon vanilla
About 6 tablespoons light brown sugar

Position a rack in the lower third of the oven and preheat the oven to 325°. Bring a kettle of water to a boil, then reduce the heat to keep it warm.

Place the cream and espresso powder in a heavy saucepan over medium heat. Heat, stirring to dissolve the powder, until the cream is steaming and just showing bubbles around the edges.

Whisk the egg yolks and sugar in a large heatproof bowl until they're completely mixed and the yolks are light yellow. Carefully whisk in a ladle of the hot cream mixture to warm the yolks. Slowly whisk in a couple of more ladles, then whisk in the remaining cream mixture. Pour through a sieve into a clean bowl to remove any lumps, bubbles, or foam. Stir in the bourbon and vanilla.

Place 6 (6-ounce) ramekins in a roasting pan. Carefully ladle the cream mixture into the ramekins, dividing it evenly. Place the roasting pan in the oven, then pour in hot water halfway up the sides of cups.

Bake for 35–40 minutes, until barely set but still jiggly in the middle. Remove from the oven and let stand for 20 minutes, then remove the ramekins from the roasting pan and place on a rack to cool for 1 hour. (To make it easier to lift them, wrap rubber bands around the ends of a set of tongs so the dishes won't slip.)

Chill for several hours or overnight. Sprinkle about 1 tablespoon light brown sugar over each brûlée and either use a kitchen torch or place under a broiler to melt and brown the sugar.

Bourbon-Butterscotch Sauce

The "scotch" in "butterscotch" is believed to have come from an old term for score, or cut into pieces, not from the whiskey. But my favorite flavor of Lifesavers has always been butter rum, so it seemed to me that bourbon, butter, and sugar needed to come together. Use this sauce over ice cream or warm cake or bread pudding—or give into temptation and just eat it by the spoonful.

MAKES ABOUT 2 CUPS

---

4 tablespoons unsalted butter
1 cup packed dark brown sugar
¾ cup heavy cream
1 teaspoon vanilla
1 tablespoon bourbon
½ teaspoon kosher salt

Melt the butter over medium heat in a 2-quart saucepan. Add the brown sugar and stir until the sugar and butter are completely mixed and look wet. Reduce the heat to medium-low and continue cooking, stirring occasionally, until the sugar is melted, about 5 minutes. (It may still look a little like wet sand, but that's OK. Don't burn it by trying to completely melt it.)

Whisk in the cream until completely blended. Increase the heat to medium and cook, whisking occasionally, for 10 minutes.

Remove from the heat and cool for 10 minutes. Pour into a heatproof bowl and stir in the vanilla, bourbon, and salt.

Cover and refrigerate for up to 1 week. Reheat in the microwave for 1–2 minutes, stirring to soften, before using.

Bourbon-Pecan Pie

The butterscotch chips bring out the caramel flavor of the bourbon in this pie. If you really need chocolate, though, you can replace the butterscotch chips with chocolate chips.

MAKES 8 SERVINGS

---

1 unbaked 9-inch pie crust

2 eggs

1 cup sugar

1 stick unsalted butter, melted and cooled

2 tablespoons bourbon

1/4 cup cornstarch

1 cup chopped pecans

1/2 cup butterscotch chips

Preheat the oven to 350°. Line a pie plate with the pie crust, easing it into the bottom. Turn the edges under and crimp to make an edge.

Whisk the eggs well in a mixing bowl. Gradually whisk in the sugar, mixing well. Whisk in the butter, bourbon, and cornstarch. Stir in the pecans and butterscotch chips, then pour the mixture into the pie crust.

Bake for 45 minutes, covering the edges of the crust with foil if it's getting too brown. Remove from the oven and cool on a wire rack. Serve with whipped cream flavored with a little bourbon or with Bourbon Cream Topping (page 88).

Bourbon-Fudge Pie

*This is a dense and very rich chocolate pie with a crispy top and a
very adult flavor. It's just the thing for the end of a dinner party.*

MAKES 12 SERVINGS

---

1 unbaked 9-inch pie crust

1½ cups pecans

8 (1-ounce) squares semisweet chocolate

4 tablespoons unsalted butter, at room temperature

1 cup packed light brown sugar

3 eggs

1 teaspoon instant espresso powder

3 tablespoons bourbon

¼ cup all-purpose flour

Preheat the oven to 375°. Line a pie plate with the pie crust,
easing it into the bottom. Turn the edges under and crimp to
make a high edge.

Spread the pecans in a dry skillet over medium heat. Toast,
stirring often, until lightly browned and fragrant. Remove from
the heat and cool, then chop coarsely.

Place the chocolate in a heatproof mixing bowl and microwave for 2 minutes, stirring every 30 seconds, until smooth.

Beat the butter and brown sugar with an electric mixer on
medium speed for 5 minutes. Add the eggs one at a time, beating well after each. Stir in the chocolate, espresso powder, bourbon, flour, and pecans.

Spoon into the pie crust and bake for 25 minutes. Remove
from the oven and cool on a wire rack. Refrigerate for at least
1 hour before serving.

Serve each slice with Bourbon Cream Topping (page 88) or
whipped cream flavored with a little bourbon.

Eugene Walter's Coffee Break Pie

Eugene Walter was a native of Mobile, Alabama, and a citizen of the world. He lived much of his life in Rome while writing about his beloved South, including the classic American Cooking: Southern Style *for a Time-Life series on regional cooking. After he died in 1998, the executor of his estate, Donald Goodman, found the manuscript for a book on cooking and drinking with spirits. It was published in 2011 as* The Happy Table of Eugene Walter: Southern Spirits in Food and Drink. *Happy table, indeed, when this sweet, simple pie finishes the meal.*

MAKES 6–8 SERVINGS

---

1 cup cold milk
1 (4-serving-size) package instant vanilla pudding mix
1 tablespoon instant coffee or instant espresso powder
2 cups frozen whipped topping, thawed, divided
3 tablespoons bourbon
1 (9-inch) graham cracker crust

Pour the milk into a mixing bowl. Add the pudding mix and coffee and whisk for 2 minutes. Gently fold in 1½ cups whipped topping and the bourbon. Spoon into the graham cracker crust.

Freeze for 2 hours or until firm. Half an hour before serving, place in the refrigerator to soften. Top with the remaining ½ cup whipped topping. Refrigerate leftovers.

Bourbon Cream Topping

Whipped cream is nice, bourbon-flavored whipped cream is even nicer, but this topping is the best. The addition of mascarpone makes it thicker, richer, and more stable than plain whipped cream. You can find mascarpone in the gourmet cheese section of your supermarket.

MAKES ABOUT 2 CUPS

¼ cup mascarpone cheese, at room temperature
1 cup heavy cream
1 tablespoon confectioners' sugar
2 tablespoons bourbon
1 teaspoon vanilla

Using an electric mixer fitted with a whisk attachment (if you don't have one, a regular beater will work just as well), beat the mascarpone until fluffy.

Add the cream and confectioners' sugar and beat on medium-high until fluffy and thick enough to show tracks. Beat in the bourbon and vanilla.

Serve immediately or cover and refrigerate for up to 3 days.

Orange-Bourbon Bundt Cake

The bourbon is in the glaze for this simple mix cake.

MAKES 12 SERVINGS

Nonstick cooking spray
1 tablespoon flour
1 (16½-ounce) package butter-flavored cake mix
11 tablespoons unsalted butter, at room temperature, divided
3 eggs
½ cup plus 2 tablespoons orange juice, divided
1 cup sugar
⅓ cup bourbon

Preheat the oven to 350°. Spray a Bundt pan with cooking spray and dust with the flour.

Combine the cake mix, 7 tablespoons butter, the eggs, and ½ cup orange juice in a mixing bowl and beat with an electric mixer on low for 1 minute, just to combine. Increase the speed to medium and beat for 4 minutes.

Scrape the batter into the prepared cake pan, smoothing the top. Bake for 35 minutes, or until the top is golden brown and springs back when touched lightly. Cool in the pan for 10 minutes.

While the cake cools, make the bourbon syrup. Combine the sugar, the remaining 2 tablespoons orange juice, and the remaining 4 tablespoons butter in a saucepan over medium heat. Cook, stirring, until the butter is melted and the sugar is dissolved. Turn off the heat and stir in the bourbon.

Turn out the cake onto a cake plate. Use a wooden or metal skewer to poke holes all around the top of the cake. Stir the glaze, then slowly spoon it over the cake, letting some of it run down the sides and into the center hole. Let it stand while the cake absorbs the syrup before slicing.

Cover and refrigerate leftovers.

Sean Brock's Bourbon- Apple Stack Cake

Charleston chef Sean Brock uses his southern background to inspire his cooking, particularly in elevating humble ingredients and traditions to new heights. His version of a stack cake, an old Appalachian dessert that uses preserved apples to create a sturdy and impressive cake, came from his grandmother, Audrey Morgan—minus the bourbon, of course. You can use a good-quality apple butter from a farmstand, or you can make your own (page 93). Making this cake is quite an undertaking, so leave a couple of days to bake all the layers and assemble the cake.

MAKES 18–20 SERVINGS

FOR THE CAKE
1 stick unsalted butter, at room temperature,
    for preparing the pans
4 teaspoons ground ginger
2 teaspoons allspice
2 teaspoons cinnamon
9 cups self-rising flour (preferably a low-protein southern
    flour, such as Southern Biscuit or White Lily)
2 cups sugar
6 large eggs
1½ cups canola oil
2 cups buttermilk
2 cups sorghum (not molasses)
1½ cups bourbon, divided
2 quarts apple butter, divided

2 cups packed light brown sugar

1 (14-ounce) can sweetened condensed milk

1 stick unsalted butter, chopped

¼ cup whole milk

1 teaspoon vanilla

Preheat the oven to 350°. Grease the bottom and sides of a 10-inch springform pan with butter, then cut a circle of parchment paper, fit it into the bottom, and butter it. (You'll need to make 5–6 layers, so use more than 1 pan if you have it. But you can bake the layers 1 at a time if needed.)

Sift the spices and flour into a very large mixing bowl. Whisk in the sugar.

In a separate large bowl, lightly beat the eggs. Gently whisk in the oil, buttermilk, and sorghum, trying not to create a lot of froth.

Slowly stir the wet ingredients into the dry ingredients until combined, using a spatula to get to the bottom of the bowl and break up any pockets of flour.

Pour ½ inch of batter into the prepared pan (the batter should be halfway up the first joint of your index finger). Bake for 15–20 minutes, until the top is golden brown and springs back when you press it. Remove from the oven and cool for 5–10 minutes.

Remove the layer from the pan, leaving the parchment paper on the bottom of the layer, and place it on a rack to cool completely. Regrease and line the pan and continue baking until you have 5–6 layers. (You can make the layers 1 day ahead, and store them, wrapped in plastic wrap, at room temperature overnight.)

Using a long, serrated knife, cut each layer in half horizontally, creating two thin layers. (You can also wrap dental floss around each layer and pull the ends together to cut it in half.) Remove the parchment paper from the bottom of each layer.

Place half of 1 layer, cut-side up, on a large, sturdy cake plate. Sprinkle the cut side with 1 tablespoon bourbon and spread with apple butter. Sprinkle the cut side of the other half with bourbon and place cut-side down on the first layer. Spread the top with apple butter.

Repeat with the remaining layers of cake, using all the bourbon and apple butter. For the final layer, sprinkle the cut side with bourbon, place it cut-side down, but do not spread apple butter on top.

To make the glaze, combine the brown sugar and sweetened condensed milk in a medium saucepan over medium heat. Cook, stirring constantly, until the sugar dissolves, about 7 minutes. (The mixture will still look very thick.)

Remove from the heat and stir in the butter a few pieces at a time until melted. When all the butter has been incorporated, stir in the milk and vanilla. Cool for 7 minutes.

Carefully pour the glaze over the top of the cake, letting it trickle down the sides. Using an icing spatula, spread the glaze evenly over the outside of the cake. Since the glaze can spread quickly, it's a good idea to place the cake plate on a baking sheet or cutting board to catch any glaze that runs off. You can scoop it up and return it to the sides of the cake.

Let the cake stand overnight or for a full day before cutting. To make it easier to cut, slice the cake in half and then cut each half-circle into tall, thin slices.

The cake will keep for 3 days at room temperature or 5 days in the refrigerator.

Apple Butter

Sean Brock grew up eating his grandmother's apple butter on bis-
cuits almost every morning. In his family, making apple butter
was a yearly ritual. He prefers using Thomas Jefferson's favorite
apple, the Newtown Pippin, although you can also use Granny
Smiths.

MAKES 2 QUARTS

12 cups unpeeled, cored, and chopped apples

¾ cup fresh apple cider

1 cup sugar

1 teaspoon cinnamon

½ teaspoon ground cloves

1 teaspoon nutmeg

2 teaspoons ground ginger

Combine the apples and cider in a slow cooker. Cover and cook
on low for 8 hours, until the apples are very soft. Purée in a food
mill or press through a sieve to remove the skins.

Place the purée in a heavy, nonreactive 3-quart pot. Add the
sugar and spices. Cover and cook over low heat for 1–2 hours. If
the apple butter isn't thick enough, increase the heat to high and
cook, watching carefully to make sure it doesn't burn. It should
be much thicker and darker than apple sauce. Cool.

Apple butter will keep for several weeks in the refrigerator or
it may be frozen indefinitely.

Lane Cake

The legendary Lane Cake was created by Emma Rylander Lane of Clayton, Alabama, in the 1890s for a baking contest in Columbus, Georgia. The original name was Prize Cake. It's become deeply ingrained in southern culture since then, most famously in Harper Lee's To Kill a Mockingbird, *where it was Miss Maudie Atkinson's specialty, "so packed with shinny, it made me tight." The original just had raisins and bourbon in the filling, but more goodies have been added over the years. The icing varies, but such a special cake deserves effort, so I use my mother's old-fashioned boiled-syrup buttercream tinted with a hint of bourbon.*

MAKES 12 SERVINGS

FOR THE CAKE
Nonstick cooking spray
3¼ cups all-purpose flour
1 tablespoon baking powder
½ teaspoon salt
1 cup milk (nonfat or reduced-fat)
1 teaspoon vanilla
8 egg whites (see Note below)
2 sticks unsalted butter, at room temperature
2 cups sugar

FOR THE FILLING
8 egg yolks
1¼ cups sugar
1 stick unsalted butter
1 cup shredded coconut (thawed frozen coconut is fine)
½ cup chopped golden raisins
1 cup chopped pecans
⅓ cup bourbon
1 teaspoon vanilla
⅛ teaspoon salt

1 cup sugar

⅛ teaspoon cream of tartar

¼ cup water

2 egg whites

1 tablespoon bourbon

¼ teaspoon vanilla

⅛ teaspoon salt

10 tablespoons plus 2 teaspoons unsalted butter,
    at room temperature

Preheat the oven to 350°. Spray 3 (8- or 9-inch) cake pans with cooking spray, then line the bottoms with parchment paper circles. Spray the paper and dust each pan with flour, knocking out the excess.

Sift the flour and then measure it into a mixing bowl. Whisk in the baking powder and salt and set aside. Stir together the milk and vanilla and set aside.

Beat the 8 egg whites with a mixer at medium speed for 1 minute, until foamy. Increase the speed and beat until the egg whites are stiff enough to hold a peak that curls over when the beaters are lifted.

Combine the butter and sugar in a large bowl and beat on high until fluffy. On low speed, beat in the flour mixture by thirds, alternating with the milk mixture and beginning and ending with flour.

Fold about a third of the beaten egg whites into the batter, then add the remainder of the egg whites, folding gently until just combined (the batter may look a little curdled).

Divide the batter evenly between the prepared pans, smoothing the tops. Bake for 20–25 minutes, until the tops are pale gold and spring back when lightly pressed. Cool in the pans for 10 minutes. Turn out onto a wire rack upside-down and carefully remove the parchment paper from the bottoms. Turn right-side up and cool completely. (You can make the layers a day ahead, wrap lightly in plastic wrap, and store at room temperature.)

To make the filling, combine the egg yolks and sugar in a mixing bowl and beat with a mixer at medium speed for 4–5 minutes, until thick, fluffy, and pale yellow. Scrape the egg yolk mixture into a double boiler or a heatproof mixing bowl set in a saucepan of simmering water. Cut the butter into chunks and add. Cook on medium heat, stirring often, for 15–20 minutes, until very thick and smooth.

Remove from the heat and stir in the coconut, raisins, and pecans. Stir in the bourbon, vanilla, and salt. Cover and chill well. (The filling may thin out when you add the bourbon, but it will thicken back up when chilled. You can also put the filling in the freezer for 30 minutes or so.)

To make the icing, in a small saucepan, combine the sugar, cream of tartar, and water. Attach a candy thermometer to the side of the pan, adjusting it so the first couple of inches of the thermometer are immersed but the tip isn't touching the bottom of the pan. Bring to a boil over medium to medium-low heat, brushing the side of the pan once or twice with water. Boil until it reaches 240° (soft-ball stage).

While the sugar is boiling, beat the 2 egg whites until they hold stiff peaks when the beaters are lifted. Working slowly, beat a little syrup at a time into the egg whites. Continue beating until the mixture forms soft peaks when the beaters are lifted. Beat in the bourbon, vanilla, and salt. Set aside to cool until the bottom of the bowl is barely warm.

In a second mixing bowl, beat the butter until fluffy. Beat in the egg white mixture a couple of tablespoons at a time, stopping the mixer for each addition, until very fluffy. (The icing can be made ahead of time and refrigerated, but let it come to room temperature before icing the cake.)

Using a long, serrated knife (or dental floss wrapped around each layer and pulled tight), cut each layer in half horizontally. Place the top half upside-down on a cake plate and spread a layer of filling on the cut side. Top with the other half and then more filling. Continue with the remaining layers, but don't spread filling on the top layer.

Spread the icing on the top and sides of the cake. Let stand for several hours or overnight before slicing.

NOTE ✳ Eggs will separate more easily at room temperature. If you don't have time to wait for them to come to room temperature, cover them with warm tap water for a few minutes. Also, with this many eggs, you don't want to risk ruining the whites with a bit of broken yolk, so use the 3 bowl method. Crack the first egg and catch the whites in one bowl, then place the yolk in a second bowl; pour the whites in a third bowl and then continue the process with the remaining eggs.

Maple-Bourbon Ice Cream

This is one time when the North and the South play well together: Maple syrup and bourbon were made to go together. Even though Grade A syrup has a higher price tag, I think Grade B is better for cooking, with a deeper, smokier flavor.

MAKES 1 QUART

1 tablespoon sugar

1½ teaspoons cornstarch

1 egg

1 cup whole milk

½ cup maple syrup, preferably Grade B
   (don't use maple-flavored pancake syrup)

½ cup bourbon

2½ cups heavy cream

Combine the sugar and cornstarch in a small saucepan and whisk to mix well; there shouldn't be any lumps. Add the egg and whisk until smooth and pale yellow. Whisk in the milk.

Place the maple syrup in a small saucepan over medium heat and cook until it just comes to a simmer. Turn off the heat.

Place the saucepan with the milk mixture over medium heat and cook, stirring constantly, until it thickens and is just starting to boil. Remove from the heat and stir in the warm syrup. Let stand at room temperature for 30 minutes, until completely cool.

Scrape the maple custard into a mixing bowl. Stir in the bourbon, then the cream. Cover with plastic wrap and refrigerate for 3 hours or overnight, until completely chilled. Freeze in an ice cream maker according to the manufacturer's instructions.

Place in an airtight container and place in the freezer several hours before serving to allow it to set up.

Acknowledgments

My thanks to Amy Preske of the Sazerac Bourbon Co.; Freddie Johnson of Buffalo Trace; Mary Ellyn Hamilton and Jean Harrison of the Oscar Getz Whiskey Museum; the staff of Barton 1792 Distilling in Bardstown, Kentucky; chefs Sean Brock of Charleston and Bill Smith of Chapel Hill; mixologist Greg Best of Holeman & Finch; John T. Edge and the whole Southern Foodways Alliance crew; Debbie Moose; Andrea Weigl; and Mark Hames. Also, I owe a huge debt of thanks to Elaine Maisner and the entire staff of the University of North Carolina Press for their trust, encouragement, and unending patience.

Index